THE CONSTITUTIONS OF THE STATES
A STATE BY STATE GUIDE
AND BIBLIOGRAPHY

THE CONSTITUTIONS

OF THE STATES
A STATE BY STATE
GUIDE AND
BIBLIOGRAPHY
to Current Scholarly Research

by
BERNARD D. REAMS, JR., J.D., Ph.D
and
STUART D. YOAK, Ph.D.

OCEANA PUBLICATIONS, INC., DOBBS FERRY, NEW YORK

Library of Congress Cataloging-in-Publication Data

Reams, Bernard D.
    The constitutions of the states: a state by state guide and bibliography to current scholarly research/by Bernard D. Reams, Jr. and Stuart D. Yoak.
        p.   cm.
    Includes indexes.
    ISBN 0-379-20970-5: $60.00
    1. United States—Constitutional law, State—Bibliography.
I. Yoak, Stuart D.   II. Title.
KF4529.R43   1988
016.34273'02—dc19
[016.3473022]   88-19621
                                                                                CIP

Manufactured in the United States of America

To our fathers
Maj. Bernard D. Reams, U.S. Army (Ret.)
and
Dale Martin Yoak
(1911-1980)

TABLE OF CONTENTS

Chapter Five

Chapter Six

Chapter Seven

Chapter Eight

Chapter Nine

Chapter Ten

Chapter Eleven

Chapter Twelve

Chapter Thirteen

Chapter Fourteen

Chapter Fifteen

Chapter Sixteen

Chapter Seventeen

Chapter Eighteen

Chapter Nineteen

Chapter Twenty

Chapter Twenty-one

Chapter Twenty-two

Chapter Twenty-three

Chapter Twenty-four

Chapter Twenty-five

Chapter Twenty-six

Chapter Twenty-seven

Chapter Twenty-eight

Chapter Twenty-nine

Chapter Thirty

Chapter Thirty-one

Chapter Thirty-two

Chapter Thirty-three

Chapter Thirty-four

Chapter Thirty-five

Chapter Thirty-six

Chapter Thirty-seven

Chapter Thirty-eight

Chapter Thirty-nine

Chapter Forty

Chapter Forty-one

Chapter Forty-two

Chapter Forty-three

Chapter Forty-four

Chapter Forty-five

Chapter Forty-six

Chapter Forty-seven

Chapter Forty-eight

Chapter Forty-nine

Chapter Fifty

Indexes

INTRODUCTION

This book is a companion volume to *The Constitution of the United States: A Guide and Bibliography to Current Scholarly Research*. The first title was initiated largely to help commemorate and participate in the increased research effort celebrating the bicentennial of the United States Constitution. Frequently during the compilation of our first work we found references to state constitutional scholarship. Many of the state constitutions have been revised and rewritten over the years, but the secondary literature and commentary surrounding these legal milestones has lagged far behind that of the federal constitution. Additionally, no comprehensive bibliography existed which compiled and organized this body of secondary literature. Our objective in this new title remained the same: to provide the legal scholar and researcher with both a guide and a bibliography to constitutional writings. Our hope is that *The Constitutions of the States: A State by State Guide and Bibliography to Current Scholarly Research* will provide direction for future researchers and in so doing open up this vast area of generally untapped resources and bring it into the fabric of the American legal world.

The Constitutions of the States focuses primarily upon current research in the legal periodical literature. The design and organizational structure follows that established with our prior work. This time each chapter is devoted to a single state constitution and within each chapter the entries are arranged according to the specific articles and sections of the respective state constitutions. This method of presentation enables the researcher to focus directly upon the specific topic areas of interest. Under each article and section the entries are then arranged in reverse chronological order and then alphabetically by the author's last name. This arrangement presents the most current and pertinent items first for the investigator's review.

We consider *The Constitutions of the States* a guide in the truest sense. As with our earlier work on the United States Constitution, what we have provided here is far more than a simple listing of entries. From the Table of Contents one can see the myriad diversity presented to the legal scholar with these fifty different state constitutions. With ratification dates which range from as far back as 1784 for New Hampshire to as recent as 1986 for Rhode Island, one sees the foundation for a broad spectrum of American legal tradition. One of the most daunting of tasks, both for the scholar and bibliographer, when confronting these fifty different constitutional documents is their lack of uniformity. Although most do follow structures and basic content of the federal constitution, there are significantly unique features in each state constitution. This is represented in the different titles given to each article and section and in the manner of their presentation. To discern the rich insight these many unique and often subtle differences imply, the researcher only needs to consult the classic *Index Digest of State Constitutions* (2d ed. 1959-1969) published by Oceana Publications to see comparative and parallel statements of provisions of all state constitutions arranged by subject.

In *The Constitutions of the States*, we have arranged the entries by state and then by article of each constitution. Additionally, we have also provided a number of different indexes which will assist the researcher. As with our previous work, we have included an Author Index and Title Index which identify each entry. All entries in the bibliography are presented following the *Uniform System of Citation* format. Consequently, only the last name of the author is entered for journal articles. The only occasions in which an author name would not be listed in the Author Index are those where the name on the entry is "Case Comment" indicating an unsigned article in a legal periodical. These entries, however, will be listed in the Title Index and Case Name Index where appropriate.

The Title Index lists all entries in the bibliography. If the entry appears more than once in the bibliography, then each of the pages will be indicated sequentially following the title of the article in the Title Index. If two or more entries use the same name in the bibliography—such as *Constitutional Law* or *Evidence*—then a separate title will be listed in the Title Index for each new and distinct citation. Titles which begin with a number such as a year or section number precede the alphabetic entries.

One of the new features we have introduced with this book is the Case Name Index. This table of cases identifies specific case names which appear in the title of entries listed in the bibliography. Although these case names do appear in the full title of each entry, they are often not at the beginning of a title and, therefore, are lost as a search reference point in the alphabetically arranged Title Index. This new index of Case Names should improve researchers access to important entries within the bibliography and provide a method for tracking the impact specific court cases have upon the development of state constitutional law.

As with our earlier work we have concentrated on current legal scholarship in the selection of entries for *The Constitutions of the States*. The beginning point for our work was with the state constitutions themselves. We conducted a thorough and exhaustive search through the textual footnotes and commentary of each of the fifty state constitutions as contained in the annotated state codes of each state. In most cases we worked with the commercially produced state codes in an effort to identify potential entries which would have analytical or expository value for the bibliography. Our primary task has been, as it was with our first work, to produce a research took that enabled scholars to narrow their investigations according to specific articles or sections of each state constitution.

Since many of the states have revised or rewritten their constitutions over the years we decided to concentrate only on the version currently in effect. The current date for each state constitution is identified in the Table of Contents chapter headings and at the beginning of each chapter. After having reviewed the fifty state constitutions, we proceeded to carefully extract potential entries from the *Index to Legal Periodicals*, *Current Law Index* and *InfoTrac* from 1970 until today. In some cases where we were unable to locate any source documents for a particular state constitution we expanded our search in the legal periodical literature to include earlier entries published before 1970.

The uniqueness of this bibliography is that it brings together many relevant articles and essays previously scattered in various locations into one centralized forum. We focus primarily on legal articles analyzing, examining, and interpreting various sections of the constitutions. Researchers should find this work an excellent starting point into contemporary state constitutional law research. Additionally, no other current volume exists which has attempted such an exhaustive bibliographic survey of the literature of state constitutional law. We do, however, wish to cite to older titles which are useful in tracing the historical development of state constitutions: B. Poore, *Charters and Constitutions* (1877); F. Stimson, *The Law of the Federal and State Constitutions of the United States* (1908); F. Thorpe, *Federal and State Constitutions* (1909); C. Kettlebrough, *State Constitutions* (1918); New York Constitutional Convention Committee, 3

Reports: *Constitutions of the States and United States* (1938); B.J. Halevy, *Selective Bibliography on State Constitution Revision,* (1963); A.L. Sturm, *Selected Bibliography on State Constitutional Revisions* (1966); A.L. Sturm, *A Bibliography on State Constitutions and Constitutional Revisions, 1945-1975* (1975); C.E. Browne, *State Constitutional Conventions...1776-1959, A Bibliography* (1973), plus *Supplements* for *1959-1975* by S.R. Yarger (1976) and for *1959-1976,* with *Revisions and Amendments,* by B. Canning (1977); *State Constitutional Conventions, Commissions, and Amendments on Microfiche (1972-1980);* and the classic W.F. Swindler, *Sources and Documents of United States Constitutions* (1979) regarded by many legal researchers as the most useful historical source for state constitutions.

As with any documents of this size and scope, one encounters many debts along the way. First, we must express our wholehearted appreciation to the Editors and our friends from Oceana Publications, Inc. Special recognition goes to Ms. Diane M. Peters, second year law student at Washington University in Saint Louis, who assisted us so conscientiously throughout the preparation and data collection phases of this project. Ms. Peters has gained our highest respect and praise for her dedication and the fine quality of her work. We also wish to thank Mr. Brain Wooley, Circulation Assistant at the Washington University Freund Law Library and Karen Hunt, student assistant, who provided valuable technical and computer assistance in bringing this project to a successful conclusion. Finally, we wish to thank all of the members from the Washington University Law Library staff who suffered with us during this major bibliographic project.

THE CONSTITUTIONS OF THE STATES
A STATE BY STATE GUIDE
AND BIBLIOGRAPHY

ALABAMA

Chapter One
ALABAMA CONSTITUTION - 1901

Article I
Declaration of Rights

Knowles and McCarthy,
Parents, Psychologists and Child Custody Disputes:
Protecting the Privilege and the Children.
37 Ala. L. Rev. 391 (1986)

Comment,
Due Process and Postjudgment Enforcement
Procedures: Where Do We Stand?
37 Ala. L. Rev. 759 (1986)

Comment,
Parental Immunity in Alabama: A Rule Without a
Reason.
36 Ala. L. Rev. 599 (1985)

Comment,
A Second Bite at the Apple: Collateral Attack and
Due Process in Taylor v. Liberty National Life
Insurance Co.
36 Ala. L. Rev. 1123 (1985)

Comment,
Thy Brother's Keeper: Alabama Takes a Step
Toward Social Host Liability.
36 Ala. L. Rev. 749 (1985)

Comment,
The Eleventh Circuit's Application of the Civil
Rights Attorney's Fees Award Act of 1976.
36 Ala. L. Rev. 103 (1984)

Comment,
Douglas v. Town of Hartford: The Fetus as
Plaintiff Under Section 1983.
35 Ala. L. Rev. 397 (1984)

Comment,
Boone v. Mullendore: Confusion   of   Actions   in
Wrongful   Life,   Wrongful   Birth,   and   Wrongful
Pregnancy.
35 Ala. L. Rev. 179 (1984)

Comment,
Title VII: Relief   for   Sexual   Harassment   in   the
Eleventh Circuit.
35 Ala. L. Rev. 193 (1984)

Comment,
Identification   of   Anonymous   Callers   Through
Circumstantial Evidence: May I Say Who's Calling,
Please?
36 Ala. L. Rev. 335 (1984)

Gamble, Howard and McElroy,
The Turncoat or Chameleonic Witness: Use of His
Prior Inconsistent Statement.
34 Ala. L. Rev. 1 (1983)

Article III
Distribution of Powers of Government

Comment,
The Vacation of Streets and Alleys in Alabama: A
Judicial Detour From Legislative Intent.
36 Ala. L. Rev. 627 (1985)

Article IV
Legislative Department

Comment,
Coemployee Immunity: The Legislature Has Spoken;
Will the Court Reply?
36 Ala. L. Rev. 649 (1985)

Schroeder,
Evidentiary Use in Criminal Cases of Collateral
Crimes and Acts: A Comparison Of the Federal
Rules and Alabama Law.
35 Ala. L. Rev. 241 (1984)

Article VI
Judicial Department

Gamble,
Opening of Court Ceremony Appellate Courts of
Alabama.
48 Ala. Law. 26 (1987)

Nagel, Beeman and Reed,
Optimum Sequencing of Court Cases to Reduce
Delay.
37 Ala. L. Rev. 583 (1986)

Comment,
Whitehead v. Johnston: The Alabama Supreme Court
and the Mother Hubbard Clause.
37 Ala. L. Rev. 699 (1986)

Alpert and Haas,
Judicial Rulemaking and the Fourth Amendment:
Cars, Containers, and Exclusionary Justice.
35 Ala. L. Rev. 23 (1984)

Graham,
Section 13: Constitutional Armor for the Common
Law.
35 Ala. L. Rev. 127 (1984)

Hoffman,
Judicial Review of Administrative Decisions in
Alabama.
35 Ala. L. Rev. 441 (1984)

Martin,
Appellate Court Workload More Than Tripok,
Employment at Will: The "American Rule" and its
Application in Alaska.
2 Arizona L. Rev. 23 (1985)

Stern,
Presumptive Sentencing in Alaska.
2 Alaska L. Rev. 227 (1985)

Comment,
Alaska's Right to Privacy Ten Years After Ravin v.
State: Developing a Jurisprudence of Privacy.
2 Alaska L. Rev. 159 (1985)

Comment,
Alaska Pacific Assurance Co. v. Brown: The Right
to Travel and the Constitutionality of Continuous
Residency Requirements.
2 Alaska L. Rev. 339 (1985)

Stern,
Consciousness of Wrongdoing: Mens Rea in Alaska.
1 Alaska L. Rev. 1 (1984)

Comment,
Visitation   Rights   for   Natural   Parents   After
Stepparent Adoption.
1 Alaska L. Rev. 319 (1984)

Comment,
The   Indian   Child   Welfare   Act: Does   It   Cover
Custody Disputes Among Extended Family Members?
1 Alaska L. Rev. 157 (1984)

Comment,
Alaska   Supreme   Court   and   the   Rights   of   Public
School   Teachers   as   Employees: A   Suggested
Response   to   Judicial   Limitation   of   Commissioner:
The   Supreme   Court   Applies   the   Gift   Tax   to
Interest-Free Loans.
35 Ala. L. Rev. 553 (1984)

Article XII
Corporations

Comment,
Sanjay, Inc. v. Duncan Construction Co.:   Alabama
Refuses Equity's Knock and Closes Another Door on
Unqualified Foreign Corporations.
36 Ala. L. Rev. 715 (1985)

Comment,
Piercing the Corporate Veil in Alabama: In Search
of a Standard.
35 Ala. L. Rev. 311 (1984)

Article XIV
Education

Comment,
Abston v. Woodard: Can the Nonrenewal of
Nontenured Teachers by Local School Boards Pass
the Mt. Healthy Test?
36 Ala. L. Rev. 355 (1984)

Comment,
Jaffree v. Board of School Commissioners: An
Interpretivist Challenge.
34 Ala. L. Rev. 657 (1983)

ALASKA

Chapter Two
ALASKA CONSTITUTION - 1959

Article I
Declaration of Rights

Wise,
Northern Lights - Equal Protection Analysis In
Alaska.
3 Alaska L. Rev. 1 (1986)

Crook,
Employment at Will: The "American Rule" and its
Application in Alaska.
2 Arizona L. Rev. 23 (1985)

Stern,
Presumptive Sentencing in Alaska.
2 Alaska L. Rev. 227 (1985)

Comment,
Alaska's Right to Privacy Ten Years After Ravin v.
State: Developing a Jurisprudence of Privacy.
2 Alaska L. Rev. 159 (1985)

Comment,
Alaska Pacific Assurance Co. v. Brown: The Right
to Travel and the Constitutionality of Continuous
Residency Requirements.
2 Alaska L. Rev. 339 (1985)

Stern,
Consciousness of Wrongdoing: Mens Rea in Alaska.
1 Alaska L. Rev. 1 (1984)

Comment,
Visitation Rights for Natural Parents After
Stepparent Adoption.
1 Alaska L. Rev. 319 (1984)

Comment,
The Indian Child Welfare Act: Does It Cover
Custody Disputes Among Extended Family Members?
1 Alaska L. Rev. 157 (1984)

Comment,
Alaska Supreme Court and the Rights of Public
School Teachers as Employees: A Suggested
Response to Judicial Limitation of Collective
Bargaining Rights.
1 Alaska L. Rev. 79 (1984)

Article II
The Legislature

Crook,
Employment at Will: The "American Rule" and its
Application in Alaska.
2 Arizona L. Rev. 23 (1985)

Fossey,
Meiners v. Bering Strait School District and the
Recall of Public Officers: A Proposal for
Legislative Reform.
2 Alaska L. Rev. 41 (1985)

Comment,
Defining an "Investment Contract" for Purposes of
Alaska Blue Sky Law: Have the Alaska Courts
Stretched Their Test Beyond Meaningful
Application?
3 Alaska L. Rev. 371 (1985)

Article IV
The Judiciary

Parks,
The Evaluation of Earnings Loss in Alaska Courts:
The Implications of Beaulieu and Guinn.
3 Alaska L. Rev. 311 (1985)

Comment,
Defining an "Investment Contract" for Purposes of
Alaska Blue Sky Law: Have the Alaska Courts
Stretched Their Test Beyond Meaningful
Application?
3 Alaska L. Rev. 371 (1985)

Burke,
Alaska (State of the Judiciary Address).
8 St. Ct.J. 15 (1984)

Fossey,
Employment Discrimination Law--Strand v.
Petersburg Public School and Fridriksson v. Alaska
USA Federal Credit Union: The Supreme Court
Charts an Uncertain Course.
1 Alaska L. Rev. 53 (1984)

Comment,
Defining "Reckless Disregard" in Defamation Suits:
The Alaska Supreme Court Renders a Narrow
Interpretation of the New York Times Rule.
1 Alaska L. Rev. 297 (1984)

Comment,
Alaska Supreme Court and the Rights of Public
School Teachers as Employees: A Suggested
Response to Judicial Limitation of Collective
Bargaining Rights.
1 Alaska L. Rev. 79 (1984)

Schept,
Alaska Bar Oks State Review.
3 Nat. L.J. 3 (1980)

Article VII
Health, Education, and Welfare

Fossey,
Meiners v. Bering Strait School District and the
Recall of Public Officers: A Proposal for
Legislative Reform.
2 Alaska L. Rev. 41 (1985)

Comment,
Alaska's "Quasi-Public" Hospitals: The Implications
of Storrs.
2 Alaska L. Rev. 185 (1985)

Comment,
Alaska Supreme Court and the Rights of Public
School Teachers as Employees: A Suggested
Response to Judicial Limitation of Collective
Bargaining Rights.
1 Alaska L. Rev. 79 (1984)

Comment,
Eidelson v. Archer: Exhaustion of Remedies in a
Private Hospital.
1 Alaska L. Rev. 277 (1984)

Article VIII
Natural Resources

Comment,
Standing to Challenge the Disposition of Land in
Alaska: A Proposed Remedy for the Inadequacies in
the Current Case Law.
3 Alaska L. Rev. 393 (1985)

Jones,
Major Issues in Developing Alaska's Outer
Continental Shelf Oil and Gas Resources.
1 Alaska L. Rev. 209 (1984)

Comment,
Mandatory Mediation of Coastal Zone Planning
Disputes in Alaska -An Innovative Approach to
Administrative Decision Making.
1 Alaska L. Rev. 349 (1984)

Comment,
Managing Sensitive Ecosystems: Honsinger v. State
and the Need For Flexibility in the Rules of Real
Property.
1 Alaska L. Rev. 117 (1984)

Comment,
Hammond v. North Slope Borough: The Endangered
Species Issue--An Exercise in Judicial Lethargy.
1 Alaska L. Rev. 129 (1984)

ARIZONA

Chapter Three
ARIZONA CONSTITUTION - 1910

Article II
Declaration of Rights

Berch,
An Essay on the Role of the Supreme Court in the
Adjudication of Constitutional Rights.
1984 Ariz. St. L.J. (1984)

Lacey,
The Struggle Over Deregulation of Religiously-
affiliated Institutions.
26 Ariz. L. Rev. 615 (1984)

Levine,
Preliminary Procedural Protection for the Press:
Jurisdiction in Distant Forums.
1984 Ariz. St. L.J. 459 (1984)

Neuborne,
Judicial Review and Fundamental Rights: A
Response to Professor Lee.
26 Ariz. L. Rev. 5 (1984)

Riggs,
Indecency on the Cable: Can It Be Regulated?
26 Ariz. L. Rev. 269 (1984)

Ryers,
The Suspect Context: A New Suspect Classification
Doctrine For The Mentally Handicapped.
26 Ariz. L. Rev. 204 (1984)

Comment,
State Equal Rights Amendments: Models for the
Future.
1984 Ariz. St. L.J. 693 (1984)

Bainton,
State Regulation of Private Religious Schools and
the State's Interest in Education.
25 Ariz. L. Rev. 123 (1983)

Berger,
The Per Se Takings Rule of Loretto V. Teleprompter
Manhattan CATV Corp.:   Access for CATV Meets
the Taking Clause.
25 Ariz. L. Rev. 689 (1983)

Malone,
Propriety of Inquiries into the Numerical Division
of a Jury.
25 Ariz. L. Rev. 525 (1983)

Wheeler,
The Right to Use Groundwater in Arizona After
Chino Valley II and Cherry v. Steiner.
25 Ariz. L. Rev. 473 (1983)

Wiese,
Eminent Domain: Admissibility of Planned Uses For
Condemnation Valuation.
25 Ariz. L. Rev. 761 (1983)

Zenoff,
What We Know, What We Think We Know, and What
We Don't Know About Women Law Professors.
25 Ariz. L. Rev. 869 (1983)

Comment,
Tantinen v. Superior Court: Arizona's Civil Courts
Remain Closed to the Indigent.
25 Ariz. L. Rev. 178 (1983)

Comment,
Propriety of Inquiries into the Numerical Division
of a Jury.
25 Ariz. L. Rev. 525 (1983)

Comment,
Compulsory Process and the Scope of the
Government's Duty to Aid in the Availability of
Defense Witnesses.
25 Ariz. L. Rev. 192 (1983)

Buchanan,
The Constitution and the Anomaly of the Pregnant
Teenager.
24 Ariz. L. Rev. 553 (1982)

Comment,
Nunchakus and the Right to Bear Arms in Arizona.
24 Ariz. L. Rev. 134 (1982)

Comment,
Ban on Police-Initiated Interrogation Following an
Accused's Invocation of His Right to Counsel.
23 Ariz. L. Rev. 1391 (1982)

Comment,
Book Banning in Public School: Don't Tinker With
Tinker.
1982 Ariz. St. L.J. 939 (1982)

Bush,
Expectation of Privacy Analysis and Warrantless
Trash Reconnaissance After Katz v. United States.
23 Ariz. L. Rev. 283 (1981)

Farren,
Common Law Right of Access to Judicial Records-
Criminal Defendant's Right to a Fair Trial.
1981 Ariz. St. L.J. 843 (1981)

Karolczyk,
Defense Witness Immunity Grants: Independent
Judicial Authority to Effectuate the Rights of
Criminal Defendants.
1981 Ariz. St. L.J. 778 (1981)

Laurence,
The Indian Commerce Clause.
23 Ariz. L. Rev. 203 (1981)

Lieberman,
Investigation of Facts in Preparation for Plea
Bargaining.
1981 Ariz. St. L.J. 557 (1981)

Lowenthal,
Adequacy of Criminal Defense Lawyers' Preparation
for Sentencing.
1981 Ariz. St. L.J. 585 (1981)

Lowenthal,
Adequacy of Fact Investigation in Criminal Defense
Lawyers' Trial Preparation.
1981 Ariz. St. L.J. 523 (1981)

Lowenthal,
Theoretical Notes on Criminal Lawyer Competency
and an Overview of the Phoenix Criminal Lawyer
Study.
1981 Ariz. St. L.J. 451 (1981)

Stein,
A Sect Apart: A History of the Legal Troubles of
the Shakers.
23 Ariz. L. Rev. 735 (1981)

Thomas,
Preventing Non-Profit Profiteering: Regulating
Religious Cult Employment Practices.
23 Ariz. L. Rev. 1003 (1981)

Comment,
Destruction of Criminal Evidence.
23 Ariz. L. Rev. 460 (1981)

Comment,
Regulation of Potentially Protected Expression
Through The Control of Liquor Dispensation.
23 Ariz. L. Rev. 395 (1981)

Comment,
Protecting Access to the Criminal Court.
1981 Ariz. St. L.J. 1049 (1981)

Bolton,
Constitutional Limitations on Restricting Corporate
and Union Political Speech.
22 Ariz. L. Rev. 373 (1980)

Kiley,
PACing the Burger Court: The Corporate Right to
Speak and the Public Right to Hear After First
National Bank v. Bellotti.
22 Ariz. L. Rev. 427 (1980)

Maltz,
Illegitimacy and Equal Protection.
1980 Ariz. St. L.J. 831 (1980)

Comment,
In Search of a Standard Governing Investigative Detainments.
22 Ariz. L. Rev. 211 (1980)

Comment,
Witness' Fifth Amendment Privilege at Odds with Defendant's Sixth Amendment Right of Confrontation.
22 Ariz. L. Rev. 1108 (1980)

Comment,
Jurisdiction over Nonmember Indians on Reservations.
1980 Ariz. State L.J. 727

Comment,
Equal Protection and Statutory Rape Legislation.
22 Ariz. L. Rev. 1078 (1980)

Article III
Distribution of Powers

Comment,
Constitutional Analysis of Legislative Review of Agency Rules.
2 Ariz. St. L.J. 493 (1985)

Lee,
Preserving Separation of Powers: A Rejection of Judicial Legislation through the Fundamental Rights Doctrine.
25 Ariz. L. Rev. 805 (1983)

Article VI
Judicial Department

Pulaski,
Capital Sentencing in Arizona: A Critical Evaluation.
1984 Ariz. B.J. 1 (1984)

Freeman,
Arizona Civil Appellate Procedure - An Update.
1983 Ariz. St. L.J. 483 (1983)

Prentice,
Supreme Court Rhetoric.
25 Ariz. L. Rev. 85 (1983)

Ulrich,
Court Improvement in Arizona..
1983 Ariz. St. L.J. 483 (1983)

Abraham,
A Comment on Three Fallacies of Interpretation:
Precedent and Judicial Decision.
23 Ariz. L. Rev. 771 (1981)

Comment,
Jurisdiction over Nonmember Indians on
Reservations.
3 Ariz. St. L.J. 727 (1980)

Article VII
Suffrage and Elections

Comment,
Tax Increment Financing, Constitutionality in Light
of Arizona Voter Approval Requirements.
24 Ariz. L. Rev. 107 (1982)

Article IX
Public Debt, Revenue, and Taxation

Comment,
Arizona Adopts an "Equitable and Reasonable
Consideration" Test to Identify Gifts of Public
Funds to Private Entities.
27 Ariz. L. Rev. 579 (1985)

Comment,
Tax Increment Financing, Constitutionality in Light
of Arizona Voter Approval Requirements.
24 Ariz. L. Rev. 107 (1982)

Article XI
Education

Bainton,
State Regulation of Private Religious Schools and
State's Interest in Education.
25 Ariz. L. Rev. 123 (1983)

Comment,
Book Banning in Public Schools: Don't Tinker With
Tinker.
1982 Ariz. St. L.J. 939 (1982)

Article XIII
Municipal Corporations

Pearce,
Quasi-Municipal Water Districts In Arizona: A
Review of Statutory Formulae.
23 Ariz. L. Rev. 883 (1981)

Comment,
City Sign Ordinances Not Enacted in Accordance
with State Requirements.
22 Ariz. L. Rev. 1179 (1980)

Article XIV
Corporations Other Than Municipal

Hovenkamp,
Predatory Pricing and the Ninth Circuit.
1983 Ariz. St. L.J. 443 (1983)

Comment,
Service of Process on Corporation's Ostensible
Agent.
22 Ariz. L. Rev. 1057 (1980)

Article XV
Corporation Commission

Comment,
Judicial Review of Rate Decisions Under Arizona's
Bifurcated Statute.
23 Ariz. L. Rev. 1301 (1982)

Article XVIII
Labor

Hermann,
Property Rights In One's Job: The Case for
Limiting Employment-At-Will.
24 Ariz. L. Rev. 763 (1982)

Crossman,
Establishment of the Average Monthly Wage,
"Injury" means "Disability" in Arizona's Workmen's
Compensation Statute.
1980 Ariz. St. L.J. 853 (1980)

Simpson,
The Parental Claim for Loss of Society
Companionship Resulting From the Negligent Injury
of a Child: A Proposal For Arizona.
1980 Ariz. St. L.J. 909 (1980)

Comment,
Bartlett's Prickly Pair (Contributory Negligence and
Assumption of Risk): Need Plaintiffs Be "Stuck"
With Both?
22 Ariz. L. Rev. 1156 (1980)

Comment,
Torts-Bystander Recovery in Arizona For Negligent
Infliction of Emotional Distress.
1980 Ariz. St. L.J. 981 (1980)

Article XX
Ordinance

Lobsenz,
"Dependent Indian Communities:" A Search For A
Twentieth Century Definition.
24 Ariz. L. Rev. 1 (1982)

Comment,
The Extension of Arizona's Workmen's Compensation
Act to The Navajo Reservation: An Unjustified
Infringement of Sovereignty?
24 Ariz. L. Rev. 168 (1982)

Comment,
Jurisdiction   Over   Nonmember   Indians   on
Reservations.
1980 Ariz. St. L.J. 727 (1980)

Article XXV
Right to Work

Axford,
Fired "At Will," Search For a Remedy.
18 Ariz. B.J. 22 (1983)

ARKANSAS

Chapter Four
ARKANSAS CONSTITUTION - 1874

Article II
Declaration of Rights

Gitelman and McIvor,
Domicile, Residence and Going to School in
Arkansas.
37 Ark. L. Rev. 843 (1984)

Wright,
Damages or Compensation for Unconstitutional Land
Use Regulations.
37 Ark. L. Rev. 612 (1984)

Comment,
White v. Gladden: A Change in law of Damages or
a Change in Evidentiary Burden?
37 Ark. L. Rev. 718 (1984)

Comment,
KARK-TV v. Simon: The Current Status of the
"Fair Report" Privilege in Arkansas.
38 Ark. L. Rev. 181 (1984)

Comment,
The Free Press-Fair Trial Controversy: A New
Standard for Closure Motions in Criminal
Proceedings.
38 Ark. L. Rev. 403 (1984)

Comment,
Dupree v. Alma School District No. 30: Mandate for
an Equitable State Aid Formula.
37 Ark. L. Rev. 1019 (1984)

Comment,
Missouri v. Hunter and the Legislature: Double
Punishment Without Double Jeopardy.
37 Ark. L. Rev. 1000 (1984)

Kennon,
Legislation of the 1983 General Assembly, Criminal
Law.
6 U. Ark. Little Rock L.J. 613 (1983)

Comment,
Constitutional Law – Due Process – Arkansas'
Sunday Closing Law is Declared Unconstitutionally
Vague.
6 U. Ark. Little Rock L.J. 305 (1983)

Comment,
Attwood v. Estate of Attwood: A Partial
Abrogation of the Parental Immunity Doctrine.
36 Ark. L. Rev. 451 (1983)

Comment,
Speedy Trial and Excludable Delays Under the
Arkansas Rules of Criminal Procedure: Norton v.
State.
35 Ark. L. Rev. 591 (1982)

Comment,
Divorce and the Division of Marital Property in
Arkansas - Equal or Equitable?
35 Ark. L. Rev. 671 (1982)

Naramore,
Survey of Arkansas Law: Constitutional Law.
4 U.Ark. Little Rock L.J. 179 (1981)

Comment,
Constitutional Law - Equal Protection and School
Funding In Arkansas, Dupree v. Alma School Dist.
No. 30.
6 U. Ark. Little Rock L.J. 541 (1983)

Farrow,
New Jersey v. Portash: The Scope of Testimonial
Competency and Privilege.
34 Ark. L. Rev. 306 (1980)

Jans,
Survey of Constitutional Law.
3 U. Ark. Little Rock L.J. 184 (1980)

Sallings,
Survey of Arkansas Law.
3 U. Ark. Little Rock L.J. 277 (1980)

Article IV
Departments

Watkins,
Open Meetings Under the Arkansas Freedom of
Information Act.
38 Ark. L. Rev. 268 (1984)

Powers,
Separation of Powers: The Unconstitutionality of
the Arkansas Legislative Council.
36 Ark. L. Rev. 124 (1982)

Gingerich,
Mandamus of Unexecuted Executive Discretionary
Powers.
33 Ark. L. Rev. 765 (1980)

Jans,
Survey of Constitutional Law.
3 U. Ark. Little Rock L.J. 184 (1980)

Article V
Legislative Department

Watkins,
Access to Public Records under the Arkansas
Freedom of Information Act.
37 Ark. L. Rev. 741 (1984)

Powers,
Separation of Powers: The Unconstitutionality of
the Arkansas Legislative Council.
35 Ark. L. Rev. 124 (1983)

Lowther,
Survey of Arkansas Law - Public Law.
4 U. Ark. Little Rock L.J. 243 (1981)

Article VI
Executive Department

Jeffrey, Nelson, Nunnally and Robertson,
Arkansas Law Survey, Constitutional Law.
7 U. Ark. Little Rock L.J. 179 (1984)

Powers,
Separation of Powers: The Unconstitutionality of
the Arkansas Legislative Council.
36 Ark. L. Rev. 124 (1982)

Lowther,
Survey of Arkansas Law - Public Law.
4 U. Ark. Little Rock L.J. 243 (1981)

Article VII
Judicial Department

Laurance,
A Very Short Article on the Precedential Value of
the Opinions from an Equally Divided Court.
37 Ark. L. Rev. 418 (1984)

Casey,
Arkansas Juvenile Courts: Do Law Judges Satisfy
Due Process In Delinquency Cases?
6 U. Ark. Little Rock L.J. 501 (1983)

Comment,
The Writ of Prohibition in Arkansas.
36 Ark. L. Rev. 256 (1982)

Brill,
The Arkansas Supreme Court Committee on
Professional Conduct 1969-1979: A Call for Reform.
33 Ark. L. Rev. 571 (1980)

Gingerich,
Mandamus of Unexecuted Executive Discretionary
Powers.
33 Ark. L. Rev. 165 (1980)

Heller and Sallings,
Survey of Public Law.
3 U. Ark. Little Rock L.J. 296 (1980)

Shively,
Survey of Family Law.
3 U. Ark. Little Rock L.J. 223 (1980)

Walsh,
The Judicial Article of the Proposed 1980
Constitution.
14 Ark. Law.Q. 206 (1980)

Article IX
Exemption

Dendy,
Survey of Arkansas Law: Business Law.
4 U. Ark. Little Rock L.J. 161981)

Comment,
Constitutional Law-Equal Protection-Arkansas'
Gender-Based Statutes on Dower, Election, Statutory
Allowances, and Homestead are Unconstitutional.
Hess v. Wims.....
4 U. Ark. Little Rock L.J. 361 (1981)

Brantley and Effland,
Inheritance, The Share of the Surviving Spouse, and
Wills: Arkansas Law and the Uniform Probate Code
Compared.
3 U. Ark. Little Rock L.J. 361 (1980)

Shively,
Survey of Family law.
3 U. Ark. Little Rock L.J. 223 (1980)

Article XII
Municipal and Private Corporations

Waddell,
Legislation of the 1983 General Assembly, Taxation.
6 U. Ark. Little Rock L.J. 636 (1983)

Jans,
Survey of Constitutional Law.
3 U. Ark. Little Rock L.J. 14 (1980)

Article XIV
Education

Gitelman and McIvor,
Domicile, Residence and Going to School in
Arkansas.
37 Ark. L. Rev. 843 (1984)

Comment,
Dupree v. Alma School District No. 30: Mandate for
an Equitable State Aid Formula.
37 Ark. L. Rev. 1079 (1984)

Comment,
Constitutional Law - Equal Protection and School
Funding in Arkansas, Dupree v. Alma School Dist.
No. 30....
6 U. Ark. Little Rock L.J. 541 (1983)

Article XVI
Finance and Taxation

Waddell,
Legislation of the 1983 General Assembly, Taxation.
6 U. Ark. Little Rock L.J. 636 (1983)

Lowther,
Survey of Arkansas Law: Public Law.
4 U. Ark. Little Rock L.J. 243 (1981)

Gingerich,
Mandamus of Unexecuted Executive Discretionary
Powers.
33 Ark. L. Rev. 765 (1980)

Article XIX
Miscellaneous Provisions

Barrier,
Usury in Arkansas: The 17% Solution.
37 Ark. L. Rev. 572 (1984)

Jeffrey, Nelson, Nunnally and Robertson,
Arkansas Law Survey, Constitutional Law.
7 U. Ark. Little Rock L.J. 179 (1984)

Dendy,
Survey of Arkansas: Business Law.
6 U. Ark. Little Rock L.J. 73 (1983)

Waddell,
Legislation of the 1983 General Assembly: Family
Law.
6 U. Ark. Little Rock L.J. 624 (1983)

Waddell,
Legislation of the 1983 General Assembly: Taxation.
6 U. Ark. Little Rock L.J. 636 (1983)

Powers,
Separation of Powers: The Unconstitutionality of
the Arkansas Legislative Council.
36 Ark. L. Rev. 124 (1982)

Comment,
The Writ of Prohibition in Arkansas.
36 Ark. L. Rev. 256 (1982)

Clark,
The Close-Connectedness Doctrine: Preserving
Consumer Rights in Credit Transactions.
33 Ark. L. Rev. 490 (1980)

Clark,
Interpretation of the Arkansas Usury Law: A
Continuation of a Conservative Trend.
33 Ark. L. Rev. 518 (1980)

Heller and Sallings,
Survey of Public Law.
3 U. Ark. Little Rock L.J. 296 (1980)

Henderson,
The Broadened Power of national Banks Regarding
Interest Rates on Credit Card Transactions.
3 U. Ark. Little Rock L.J. 115 (1980)

Tyler,
Survey of Business Law.
3 U. Ark. Little Rock L.J. 149 (1980)

Amendments to the Constitution

Gitelman and McIvor,
Domicile, Residence and Going to School in
Arkansas.
37 Ark. L. Rev. 843 (1984)

Laurence,
A Very Short Article on the Precedential Value of
the Opinions from an Equally Divided Court.
37 Ark. L. Rev. 418 (1984)

Looney,
Modification of Arkansas Water Law: Issues and
Alternatives.
38 Ark. L. Rev. 221 (1984)

Sallings,
Survey of Arkansas Law, Miscellaneous.
6 U. Ark. Little Rock L.J. 187 (1983)

Comment,
Property-Zoning -- The Courts Further Define Their
Limited Role. City of Little Rock v. Breeding.....
5 U. Ark. Little Rock L.J. 279 (1982)

Comment,
Eaton and Benton v. Supreme Court of Arkansas
Committee on Professional Conduct: Restrictions on
Legal Advertising.
35 Ark. L. Rev. 549 (1981)

Brill,
The Arkansas Supreme Court Committee on
Professional Conduct 1969-1979: A Call for Reform.
33 Ark. L. Rev. 571 (1980)

Gingerich,
Mandamus of Unexecuted Executive Discretionary
Powers.
33 Ark. L. Rev. 765 (1980)

CALIFORNIA

Chapter Five
CALIFORNIA CONSTITUTION - 1879

Article I
Declaration of Rights

McDowell,
Exclusion of Probation Revocation Hearing
Testimony from the Subsequent Trial.
13 Pepperdine L. Rev. 505 (1986)

Simon,
Rebuilding the Wall Between Church and State:
Public sponsorship of Religious Displays Under the
Federal and California Constitutions.
37 Hastings L.J. 499 (1985-1986)

Bedsworth,
In Re Lance W.: The Ship of State Makes a Course
Correction.
13 W. St. U.L. Rev. 9 (1985)

Henderson,
The Wrongs of Victim's Rights.
37 Stan. L. Rev. 937 (1985)

Gorman,
Proposition 8 Comes to Age: An Introduction.
13 W. St. U.L. Rev. 1 (1985)

Jenkins,
People v. Castro: A Road Back to Beagle and
Beyond.
13 W. St. U.L. Rev. 27 (1985)

Klein,
Proposition 8: California Law after In Re Lance W.
and People v. Castro.
12 Pepperdine L. Rev. 1059 (1985)

Kopeny,
The Impact of Proposition 8 on Statements.
13 W. St. U.L. Rev. 55 (1985)

Ryan,
Is the Two-Prong Test of Aguilar-Spinelli Alive and
Well in California?
13 W. St. U.L. Rev. 45 (1985)

Comment,
The Newsgatherer's Shield--Why Waste Space in the
California Constitution?
15 Sw. U.L. Rev. 527 (1985)

Comment,
Solem v. Helm: The Courts' Continued Struggle to
Define Cruel and Unusual Punishment.
21 Cal. W.L. Rev. 590 (1985)

Comment,
Preservation of Material Evidence in California:
Does People v. Hitch Survive California v.
Trombetta.
13 Hastings Const. L.Q. 147 (1985)

Gilbert,
The Constitution Should Protect Everyone--Even
Lawyers.
12 Pepperdine L. Rev. 75 (1984)

Anderson,
The Origins of the Press Clause.
30 UCLA L. Rev. 455 (1983)

Caso,
Nonconsensual Cal/OSHA Inspections after
Salwasser: They're Still Illegal.
14 Pac. L.J. 913 (1983)

Cochran,
California's Constitution Won't Stop Growing.
3 Cal. Law. 40 (1983)

Eberle,
Prior Restraint of Expression Through the Private
Search Doctrine.
17 U.S.F. L. Rev. 171 (1983)

Schlag,
An Attack on Categorical Approaches to Freedom of
Speech.
30 UCLA. L. Rev. 671 (1983)

Thompson,
The Constitutionality of chemical Test Presumptions
of Intoxication in Motor Vehicle Statutes.
20 San Diego L. Rev. 301 (1983)

Comment,
The Problems Facing California's New Bail Standard.
5 Glendale L. Rev. 203 (1983)

Farmer,
The Right to Jury Trial in Insurance Coverage
Declaratory Relief Actions.
13 Pac. L.J. 917 (1982)

Gerstein,
California's Constitutional Right to Privacy.
9 Hastings Int'l Const. L.Q. 385 (1982)

Goodwin,
Challenging the Private Club: Sex Discrimination
Plaintiffs Barred at the Door.
13 Sw. L. Rev. 237 (1982)

Leonard,
The Good Faith Exception to the Exclusionary Rule.
4 Whittier L. Rev. 33 (1982)

Redish,
Advocacy of Unlawful Conduct and the First
Amendment: In Defense of Clear and Present
Danger.
70 Calif. L. Rev. 1159 (1982)

Van de Kamp,
Reforming the Exclusionary Rule: An Analysis of
Two Proposed Amendments to the California
Constitution.
33 Hastings L.J. 1109 (1982)

Van de Kamp,
Response to Paul N. Halvonik. (On Exclusionary
Rule).
33 Hastings L.J. 1151 (1982)

Alleyne,
Regents   v.   Bakke: Implementing   Pre-Bakke
Admission   Policies   with   Pose-Bakke   Admissions
Procedures.
7 Black L.J. 290 (1981)

Bell,
Law School Exams and Minority-Group Students.
7 Black L.J. 304 (1981)

Clark,
Homosexual   Public   Employees: Utilizing   Section
1983 to Remedy Discrimination.
8 Hastings Const. L.Q. 255 (1981)

Freeman,
Race, Class and the Contradictions of Affirmative
Action.
7 Black L.J. 270 (1981)

Gaebler,
Union   Political   Activity   or   Collective   Bargaining?
First Amendment Limitations on the Uses of Union
Shop Funds.
14 U.C. Davis L. Rev. 591 (1981)

Goldberg,
"Interpretation" of "Due Process of Law"--a Study
in Irrelevance of Legislative History.
12 Pac. L.J. 621 (1981)

Jorde,
The   Seventh   Amendment   Right   to   Jury   Trial   of
Antitrust Issues.
69 Cal. L. Rev. 1 (1981)

Wilson,
Shifting Burdens in Criminal law: A Burden on Due
Process.
8 Hastings Const. L.Q. 731 (1981)

Comment,
Discovery   and   Administrative   Due   Process: A
Balance Between an Accused's Right to Discovery
and Administrative Efficiency.
8 Hastings Const. L.Q. 645 (1981)

Comment,
The Right to Effective Assistance of Counsel in
California: Adoption of the Sixth Amendment
"reasonably Competent Attorney" Standard.
12 Sw. U. L. Rev. 53 (1980-81)

Berrett,
"The Uncharted Area"--Commercial Speech and the
First Amendment.
13 U.C. Davis. L. Rev. 175 (1980)

Bevier,
An Informed Public, an Informing Press: The
Search for a Constitutional Principle.
68 Calif. L. Rev. 482 (1980)

Blubaugh,
California's Constitution: The Reporter's Forgotten
Ally.
55 Cal. St. B.J. 12 (1980)

Braun,
Statistics and the Law: Hypothesis Testing and its
Application to Title VII Cases.
32 Hastings L.J. 59 (1980)

Bryan,
Sexual Harassment as Unlawful Discrimination Under
Title VII of the Civil Rights Act of 1964.
14 Loy. L.A.L. Rev. 25 (1980)

Deukmejian,
"Incompetent Criminal Defense Attorney Wanted:
Needed by Guilty Defendant."
7 Orange County B.J. 39 (1980)

Creighton,
Proposition 1 and Federal Protection of State
Constitutional Rights.
75 Nw. U.L. Rev. 685 (1980)

Emerson,
First Amendment Doctrine and the Burger Court.
68 Calif. L. Rev. 422 (1980)

Frankfurt and Rodney,
California's Anti-Busing Amendment: A   Perspective
on the Now Unequal Equal Protection Clause.
10 Golden Gate U.L. Rev. 611 (1980)

Granberg,
Is Warrantless Aerial Surveillance Constitutional?
55 Calif. St. B.J. 451 (1980)

Griffith,
The Alien Meets Some Constitutional Hurdles in
Employment, Education, and Aid Programs.
17 San Diego L. Rev. 201 (1980)

Grisso,
Juveniles' Capacities to Waive Miranda Rights: An
Analysis.
68 Calif. L. Rev. 1134 (1980)

Hogue,
Chilled Bird: Freedom of Expression in the
Eighties.
14 Loy. L.A.L. Rev. 57 (1980)

Kaye,
And   Then   There   were   Twelve: Statistical
Reasoning, the Supreme Court, and the Size of the
Jury.
68 Cal. L. Rev. 1004 (1980)

Mendez,
Presumptions of Discriminatory Motive in Title VII
Treatment Cases.
32 Stan. L. Rev. 1129 (1980)

Montgomery,
Sexual Harassment in the Workplace; a Practitioner's
Guide to Tort Actions.
10 Golden Gate U.L. Rev. 879 (1980)

Needham,
The Effect of the Age Discrimination in Employment
Act Employee Benefit Plan Exception in Small
Business.
13 U.C. Davis L. Rev. 969 (1980)

Radin,
Cruel Punishment and Respect for Persons: Super
Due Process for Death.
53 S. Cal. L. Rev. 1143 (1980)

Ripple,
The Entanglement Test of the Religion Clauses--a
Ten-Year Assessment.
27 UCLA L. Rev. 1195 (1980)

Shapiro,
Remedies for Sex-Discriminatory Health and Safety
Conditions in Male-Dominated Industrial Jobs.
10 Golden Gate U.L. Rev. 1087 (1980)

Toms,
The Government's Role in the Purification of
Religious Organizations.
7 Pepperdine L. Rev. 355 (1980)

White,
Job-related Sexual Harassment and Union Women:
What are their Rights?
10 Golden Gate U.L. Rev. 929 (1980)

Wildman,
42 USCS SS1985(3) - A Private Action to Vindicate
Fourteenth Amendment Rights: A Paradox Resolved.
17 San Diego L. Rev. 317 (1980)

Wilson,
The Warrantless Automobile Search: Exception
without Justification.
32 Hastings L.J. 127 (1980)

Worthing,
"Religion" and "Religious Institutions: Under the
First Amendment.
7 Pepperdine L. Rev. 313 (1980)

Comment,
Government Protection of Church Assets from Fiscal
Abuse: The Constitutionality of Attorney General
Enforcement Under the Religion Clauses of the First
Amendment.
53 S. Cal. L. Rev. 1277 (1980)

Comment,
Article I, Section 8 of the California Constitution
and the Reasonable Accommodation Rule.
2 Whittier L. Rev. 385 (1980)

Comment,
California   Diminishes   Federally   Protected
Constitutional Property Rights.
2 Whittier L. Rev. 423 (1980)

Article II
Voting, Initiative and Referendum, and Recall

Kirsch,
Initiatives: Cutting Up The Constitution?
4 Cal. Law. 24 (1984)

Comment,
A Vote on Talleysheet is Worth Two in the Box:
Peterson v. City of San Diego.
18 U.S.F. L. Rev. 635 (1984)

Cochran,
California's Constitutional Won't Stop Growing.
3 Cal. Law. 40 (1983)

Article VI
Judicial

Comment,
Private Means to Public Ends: Implications of the
Private Judging Phenomenon in California.
17 U.C. Davis L. Rev. 611 (1984)

Comment,
Judicial Misconduct in California.
11 San Fernando L. Rev. 43 (1983)

Doorlag,
California Constitution. (California Supreme Court
Survey - A Review of Decisions: March 1981 to
May 1981)
9 Pepperdine L. Rev. 261 (1981)

Friedman,
State Supreme Courts: A Century of Style and
Citation.
33 Stan. L. Rev. 773 (1981)

MacLeod,
California Constitution and the California Suupreme
Court in Conflict Over the Harmless Error Rule.
32 Hastings L.J. 687 (1981)

Comment,
California Constitution: Article VI, 16(c): Judicial
Vacancies.
8 Pepperdine L. Rev. 575 (1981)

Creighton,
Proposition 1 and Federal Protection of State
Constitutional Rights.
75 Nw. U.L. Rev. 685 (1980)

Article IX
Education

Simon,
Rebuilding the Wall Between Church and State:
Public Sponsorship of Religious Displays under the
Federal and California Constitutions.
37 Hastings L.J. 499 (1985-1986)

Creighton,
Proposition 1 and Federal Protection of State
Constitutional Rights.
75 Nw. U.L. Rev. 685 (1980)

Article X
Water

Smith,
Rewriting California Ground Water Law: Past
Attempts and Prerequisites to Reform.
20 Cal. W.L. Rev. 223 (1984)

Article XI
Local Government

Hiscocks,
Charter City Financing in California.
16 U.S.F. L. Rev. 603 (1982)

David,
California Cities and the Constitution of 1978:
General Laws and Municipal Affairs.
7 Hastings Const. L.Q. 843 (1980)

Article XIII A
Tax Limitation Initiative

Morris,
Proposition 13: Change in Ownership: constitutional
problems.
4 L.A. Law. 24 (1984)

Cochran,
California's Constitutional Won't Stop Growing.
3 Cal. Law. 40 (1983)

Trull,
Police and Fire Service Special Assessments Under
Proposition 13.
16 U.S.F. L. Rev. 781 (1982)

Kellogg,
Deeds That do the Job: Proposition 13.
4 L.A. Law. 33 (1981)

Manvel,
Tracing Proposition 13 Effects.
13 Tax Notes 1540 (1981)

Article XV
Usury

Harrah,
The New California Usury Law in Light of the
Monetary Control Act of 1980.
35 Bus. Law. 1053 (1980)

Lloyd,
California Does it With Interest.
34 Pers. Fin. L.Q. Rep. 111 (1980)

Article XVI
Public Finance

Simon,
Rebuilding the Wall Between Church and State:
Public Sponsorship or Religious Displays under the
Federal and California Constitutions.
37 Hastings L.J. 499 (1985-1986)

COLORADO

Chapter Six
COLORADO CONSTITUTION - 1876

Article II
Bill of Rights

Johnson,
Defending Against the Confession at Trial.
15 Colo. Law. 409 (1986)

Bloom,
United State v. Leon and Its Ramifications.
56 U. Colo. L. Rev. 247 (1985)

Johnson,
Consent Searches: A Brief Review.
14 Colo. Law. 795 (1985)

Kenney,
Veracity Challenges in Colorado: A Primer.
14 Colo. Law. 227 (1985)

Nachman,
Balancing The Government's Investigative Powers
and The Citizen's Privacy Rights.
14 Colo. Law. 947 (1985)

Schultz,
The Federal Due Process and Equal Protection
Rights of Non-Indian Civil Litigants in Tribal
courts After Santa Clara Pueblo v. Martinez.
62 Den. U.L. Rev. 761 (1985)

Comment,
Setting Boundaries for Student Due Process:
Rustad v. United States Air Force and the Right to
Counsel in Disciplinary Dismissal Proceedings.
62 Den. U.L. Rev. 109 (1985)

Comment,
Twenty Questions Does Not Yield Due Process:
Chaney v. Brown and the Continued Need to Open
Prosecutor's Files in Criminal Proceedings.
62 Den. U.L. Rev. 193 (1985)

Comment,
People v. Mitchell: The Good Faith Exception in
Colorado.
62 Den. U. L. Rev. 841 (1985)

Comment,
Austin v. Litvak, Colorado's Statute of Repose for
Medical Malpractice Claims: An Uneasy Sleep.
62 Den. U.L. Rev. 825 (1985)

Comment,
Civil Rights.
62 Den. U.L. Rev. 62 (1985)

Comment,
Constitutional Law.
62 Den. U.L. Rev. 98 (1985)

Cerruti,
The Demise of the Aguilar-Spinelli Rule: A Case
of Faulty Reception.
61 Den. L.J. 431 (1984)

Levit,
The Future of Comparable Worth Theory.
56 U. Colo. L. Rev. 99 (1984)

Comment,
The Good Faith Exception: The Seventh Circuit
Limits the Exclusionary Rule in the Administrative
Contest.
61 Den. L.J. 597 (1984)

Comment,
Mueller v. Allen: Clarifying   or   Confusing
Establishment Clause Analysis of State Aid to
Public Schools?
61 Den. L.J. 877 (1984)

Comment,
People v. Quintana: How "Probative~ Is This
Colorado Decision Excluding Evidence of Post-
Arrest Silence?
56 U. Colo. L. Rev. 157 (1984)

Comment,
People v. Sporleder: Privacy Expectations Under
the Colorado Constitution.
55 U. Colo. L. Rev. 593 (1984)

Comment,
Criminal Procedure.
61 Den. L.J. 281 (1984)

Goldsmith,
Suffering Adverse Inference From Taking the Fifth
in Civil Proceedings.
12 Colo. Law. 1445 (1983)

Gordon,
Governmental Loss or Destruction of Exculpatory
Evidence: A Due Process Violation.
12 Colo. Law. 77 (1983)

Olom,
Search Warrants, Hearsay and Probable Cause--
The Supreme Court Rewrites the Rules.
12 Colo. Law. 1250 (1983)

Rivera,
Standards of Effectiveness of Criminal Counsel.
12 Colo. Law. 264 (1983)

Schwartz,
Asserting Vested Rights in Colorado.
12 Colo. Law. 1199 (1983)

Comment,
Colorado's Approach to Searches and Seizures in
Law Offices.
54 U. Colo. L. Rev. 571 (1983)

Bender,
Incriminating Evidence: What to do With a Hot
Potato.
11 Colo. Law. 880 (1982)

Bloom,
Warrant Requirement -- The Burger Court Approach.
53 U. Colo. L. Rev. 691 (1982)

Love,
Access to Mineral Lands in Colorado.
11 Colo. Law. 870 (1982)

Richilano,
Good Faith Exception to the Exclusionary Rule:
The Fourth Amendment is Not a Technicality.
11 Colo. Law. 704 (1982)

Savitz,
Attacking the Seizure--Over-coming Good Faith.
11 Colo. Law. 2395 (1982)

Comment,
The Colorado Statutory Good-Faith Exception to the
Exclusionary Rule: A Step Too Far.
53 U. Colo. L. Rev. 809 (1982)

Comment,
Liberty vs. Equality: Congressional Enforcement
Power Under the Fourteenth Amendment.
59 Den. L.J. 417 (1982)

Comment,
Privacy Rights vs. Law Enforcement Difficulties:
The Clash of Competing Interests in New York v.
Belton.
59 Den. L.J. 793 (1982)

Comment,
Some Observations on the Swinging Courthouse
Doors of Gannett and Richmond Newspapers.
59 Den. L.J. 721 (1982)

Anderson,
Closure of Pretrial Hearings and Trials to the
Press and Public.
10 Colo. Law. 306 (1981)

Karowsky,
Colorado's ERA: Off the Pedestal and Into the
Courts.
10 Colo. Law. 1284 (1981)

Comment,
Reporter's Privilege: Pankratz v. District Court.
58 Den. L.J. 681 (1981)

Comment,
People   v.   Emmert: A   Step   Backward   for
Recreational Water Use in Colorado.
52 U. Colo. L. Rev. 247 (1981)

Comment,
Reporter's Privilege: Pankratz v. District Court.
58 Den. L.J. 681 (1981)

Comment,
Bastardizing   the   Legitimate   Child: The   Colorado
Supreme   Court   Invalidates   the   Uniform   Parentage
Act Presumption of Legitimacy in R. McG. v. J.W.
59 Den. L.J. 157 (1981)

Martin,
The Problem of Delay in the Colorado Court of
Appeals.
58 Den. L.J. 1 (1980)

Article III
Distribution of Powers

Merrick,
Standing to Sue in Colorado: A State of Disorder.
60 Den. L.J. 421 (1983)

Article V
Legislative Department

Butler,
Reapportionment, The Courts, and the Voting Rights
Act: A Resegregation of the Political Process?
56 U. Colo. L. Rev. 1 (1984)

Comment,
Referendum   and   Rezoning: Margolis   v.   District
Court.
53 U. Colo. L. Rev. 745 (1982)

Article VI
Judicial

Johnson,
Defending Against the Confession at Trial.
15 Colo. Law. 409 (1986)

Bloom,
United State v. Leon and Its Ramifications.
56 U. Colo. L. Rev. 247 (1985)

Johnson,
Consent Searches: A Brief Review.
14 Colo. Law. 795 (1985)

Kenney,
Veracity Challenges in Colorado: A Primer.
14 Colo. Law. 227 (1985)

Nachman,
Balancing The Government's Investigative Powers
and The Citizen's Privacy Rights.
14 Colo. Law. 947 (1985)

Schultz,
The Federal Due Process and Equal Protection
Rights of Non-Indian Civil Litigants in Tribal
courts After Santa Clara Pueblo v. Martinez.
62 Den. U.L. Rev. 761 (1985)

Comment,
Constitutional Law.
62 Den. U.L. Rev. 98 (1985)

Comment,
Civil Rights.
62 Den. U.L. Rev. 62 (1985)

Comment,
Setting Boundaries for Student Due Process:
Rustad v. United States Air Force and the Right to
Counsel in Disciplinary Dismissal Proceedings.
62 Den. U.L. Rev. 109 (1985)

Comment,
Twenty Questions Does Not Yield Due Process:
Chaney v. Brown and the Continued Need to Open
Prosecutor's Files in Criminal Proceedings.
62 Den. U.L. Rev. 193 (1985)

Comment,
Austin v. Litvak, Colorado's Statute of Repose for
Medical Malpractice Claims: An Uneasy Sleep.
62 Den. U.L. Rev. 825 (1985)

Comment,
People v. Mitchell: The Good Faith Exception in
Colorado.
62 Den. U. L. Rev. 841 (1985)

Cerruti,
The Demise of the Aguilar-Spinelli Rule: A Case
of Faulty Reception.
61 Den. L.J. 431 (1984)

Levit,
The Future of Comparable Worth Theory.
56 U. Colo. L. Rev. 99 (1984)

Comment,
People v. Sporleder: Privacy Expectations Under
the Colorado Constitution.
55 U. Colo. L. Rev. 593 (1984)

Comment,
Criminal Procedure.
61 Den. L.J. 281 (1984)

Comment,
The Good Faith Exception: The Seventh Circuit
Limits the Exclusionary Rule in the Administrative
Contest.
61 Den. L.J. 597 (1984)

Comment,
Mueller v. Allen: Clarifying or Confusing
Establishment Clause Analysis of State Aid to
Public Schools?
61 Den. L.J. 877 (1984)

Goldsmith,
Suffering Adverse Inference From Taking the Fifth
in Civil Proceedings.
12 Colo. Law. 1445 (1983)

Gordon,
Governmental Loss or Destruction of Exculpatory
Evidence: A Due Process Violation.
12 Colo. Law. 77 (1983)

Merrick,
Standing to Sue in Colorado: A State of Disorder.
60 Den. L.J. 421 (1983)

Olom,
Search Warrants, Hearsay and Probable Cause--
The Supreme Court Rewrites the Rules.
12 Colo. Law. 1250 (1983)

Re Mene,
Original Proceedings in the Colorado Supreme
Court.
12 Colo. Law. 413 (1983)

Rivera,
Standards of Effectiveness of Criminal Counsel.
12 Colo. Law. 264 (1983)

Schwartz,
Asserting Vested Rights in Colorado.
12 Colo. Law. 1199 (1983)

Comment,
Colorado's Approach to Searches and Seizures in
Law Offices.
54 U. Colo. L. Rev. 571 (1983)

Bender,
Incriminating Evidence: What to do With a Hot
Potato.
11 Colo. Law. 880 (1982)

Bloom,
Warrant Requirement -- The Burger Court Approach.
53 U. Colo. L. Rev. 691 (1982)

Erickson,
A Summary of Colorado Supreme Court Internal
Operating Procedures.
11 Colo. Law. 356 (1982)

Love,
Access to Mineral Lands in Colorado.
11 Colo. Law. 870 (1982)

Richilano,
Good Faith Exception to the Exclusionary Rule:
The Fourth Amendment is Not a Technicality.
11 Colo. Law. 704 (1982)

Savitz,
Attacking the Seizure--Over-coming Good Faith.
11 Colo. Law. 2395 (1982)

Comment,
Privacy Rights vs. Law Enforcement Difficulties:
The Clash of Competing Interests in New York v.
Belton.
59 Den. L.J. 793 (1982)

Comment,
The Colorado Statutory Good-Faith Exception to the
Exclusionary Rule: A Step Too Far.
53 U. Colo. L. Rev. 809 (1982)

Comment,
Some Observations on the Swinging Courthouse
Doors of Gannett and Richmond Newspapers.
59 Den. L.J. 721 (1982)

Comment,
Liberty vs. Equality: Congressional Enforcement
Power Under the Fourteenth Amendment.
59 Den. L.J. 417 (1982)

Anderson,
Closure of Pretrial Hearing and Trials to the Press
and Public.
10 Colo. Law. 306 (1981)

Simon,
Rebuilding the Wallgs and Trials to the Press and
Public.
10 Colo. Law. 306 (1981)

Comment,
Bastardizing the Legitimate Child: The Colorado
Supreme Court Invalidates the Uniform Parentage
Act Presumption of Legitimacy in R. McG. v. J.W.
59 Den. L.J. 157 (1981)

Comment,
People v. Emmert: A Step Backward for
Recreational Water Use in Colorado.
52 U. Colo. L. Rev. 247 (1981)

Comment,
Reporter's Privilege: Pankratz v. District Court.
58 Den. L.J. 681 (1981)

Comment,
The Perjurious Defendant: A Proposed Solution to
the Defense Lawyer's Conflicting Ethical
Obligations to the Court and to His Client.
59 Den. L.J. 75 (1981)

Martin,
The Problem of Delay in the Colorado Court of
Appeals.
58 Den. L.J. 1 (1980)

Article VIII
State Institutions

Massey,
Protecting the Mentally Incompetent Child's Trust
Interest From State Reimbursement Claims.
58 Den. L.J. 557 (1981)

Article IX
Education

Comment,
Rights of Handicapped Students in Disciplinary
Proceedings by Public School Authorities.
53 U. Colo. L. Rev. 367 (1982)

Article X
Revenue

Low,
Appealing Property Tax Assessments.
15 Colo. Law. 798 (1986)

Briggs,
Taxation of Colorado's Sand and Gravel Reserves.
12 Colo. Law. 927 (1983)

Israel,
Property Tax Assessments in Colorado.
12 Colo. Law. 563 (1983)

Comment,
Property Tax Incentives for Implementing Soil
Conservation Programs Under Constitutional Taxing
Limitations.
59 Den. L.J. 485 (1982)

Article XVI
Mining and Irrigation

Comment,
Principles & Law of Colorado's Nontributory Ground
Water.
62 Den. U.L. Rev. 809 (1985)

Pascoe,
Plans and Studies: The Recent Quest for a Utopia
in the Utilization of Colorado's Water Resources.
55 U. Colo. L. Rev. 391 (1984)

Comment,
Nontributary, Nondesignated Groundwater: The
Huston Decision.
56 U. Colo. L. Rev. 135 (1984)

Corker,
Sporhase v. Nebraska ex rel. Douglas: Does the
Dormant Comment Clause Really Limit the Power of
a State to Forbid (1) the Export of Water and (2)
the Creation of a Water Right for use in Another
State?
54 U. Colo. L. Rev. 393 (1983)

White,
Emerging   Relationship   Between   Environmental
Regulations and Colorado Water Law.
53 U. Colo. L. Rev. 597 (1982)

Comment,
United   States   Supreme   Court   Review   of   Tenth
Circuit Decisions.
59 Den. L.J. 397 (1982)

Dempsey,
Oil Shale and Water Quality: The Colorado
Prospectus Under Federal, State, and International
Law.
58 Den. L.J. 715 (1981)

Hannay,
Recent Developments in Colorado Groundwater Law.
58 Den. L.J. 801 (1981)

Comment,
People   v.   Emmert: A   Step   Backward   for
Recreational Water Use in Colorado.
52 U. Colo. L. Rev. 247 (1981)

Comment,
Bubb v. Christensen: The Rights of the Private
Landowner Yield to the Rights of the Water
Appropriator Under the Colorado Doctrine.
58 Den. L.J. 825 (1981)

Comment,
Town of De Beque v. Enewold: Conditional Water
Rights and Statutory Water Law.
58 Den. L.J. 837 (1981)

Comment,
Diversion as an Element of Appropriation.
57 Den. L.J. 661 (1980)

Article XX
Home Rule Cities and Towns

Kerr,
Pollution or Resources Out-of-Place -- Reclaiming
Municipal Watewater for Agricultural Use.
53 U. Colo. L. Rev. 559 (1982)

Comment,
Antitrust.
58 Den. L.J. 249 (1981)

Merson,
Cumulative Impact Assessment of Western Energy
Development: Will it Happen?
51 U. Colo. L. Rev. 551 (1980)

Article XXV
Public Utilities

Hjelmfest,
Retail Competition in the Electric Utility Industry.
60 Den. L.J. 1 (1982)

Comment,
Utility Use of Renewable Resources: Legal and
Economic Implications.
59 U. Den. L.J. 663 (1982)

CONNECTICUT

Chapter Seven
CONNECTICUT CONSTITUTION - 1965

Article I
Declaration of Rights

Comment,
Probable Cause and Informant Tips Under the Connecticut Constitution.
18 Conn. L. Rev. 887 (1986)

Comment,
State Protection of Future "Persons:" Commonwealth v. Cass.
18 Conn. L. Rev. 429 (1986)

Comment,
Containing the Irrepressible: Judicial Responses to the Problem of Pre-Deliberation Discussion Among Jurors.
18 Conn. L. Rev. 127 (1985)

Alder,
The Westfarms Mall Case: An English View.
16 Conn. L. Rev. 681 (1984)

Kay,
The Jurisprudence of the Connecticut Constitution.
16 Conn. L. Rev. 667 (1984)

Comment,
State Intervention in Parental Rights: Standards for a No-Win Situation.
16 Conn. L. Rev. 541 (1984)

Comment,
The Grudging and Crabbed Approach to Due Process for the Unwed Father: Lehr v. Robertson.
16 Conn. L. Rev. 571 (1984)

Schwartz,
Liberty and Autonomy Versus Confinement and
Commitment: The History of Legal Intervention in
Colonial Connecticut.
11 J. Psychiatry & L. 461 (1983)

Comment,
Employee Right to Active Union Representation at
Investigative Interviews: The Connecticut State
Labor Board Decision in State Department of
Education.
16 Conn. L. Rev. 179 (1983)

Barrante,
State Protection of Freedom of Speech: Cologne v.
Westfarms Associates.
58 Conn. B.J. 305 (1982)

Berdon,
Protecting Liberty and Property Under the
Connecticut and Federal Constitutions: The Due
Process Clauses.
15 Conn. L. Rev. 41 (1982)

Berdon,
Protecting the Individual Liberties Under the State
Constitution.
56 Conn. B.J. 236 (1982)

Cabranes,
The Need for Continued Federal Protection of
Individual Rights.
15 Conn. L. Rev. 31 (1982)

Collier,
The Connecticut Declaration of Rights Before the
Constitution of 1818: A Victim or Revolutionary
Redefinition.
15 Conn. L. Rev. 87 (1982)

Dorsen,
State Constitutional Law: An Introductory Survey.
15 Conn. L. Rev. 99 (1982)

Macgill,
Upon a Peak in Darien: Discovering the
Connecticut Constitution.
15 Conn. L. Rev. 7 (1982)

Margulies,
A Lawyer's View of the Connecticut Constitution.
15 Conn. L. Rev. 107 (1982)

Newman,
The "Old Federalism": Protection of Individual
Rights by State Constitutions in an Era of Federal
Court Passivity.
15 Conn. L. Rev. 21 (1982)

Satter,
Litigation Under the Connecticut Constitution-
Developing a Sound Jurisprudence.
15 Conn. L. Rev. 41 (1982)

Comment,
Jury Award Advertising--Political Speech or
Commercial Speech?
15 Conn. L. Rev. 273 (1982)

Comment,
Beating the Odds: Compulsive Gambling as an
Insanity Defense--State v. Lafferty.
14 Conn. L. Rev. 341 (1982)

Comment,
Wrongful Death and Loss of Consortium in
Connecticut.
14 Conn. L. Rev. 631 (1982)

Comment,
No-Frills Due Process--Who Needs Counsel?:
Lassiter v. Department of Social Services.
14 Conn. L. Rev. 733 (1982)

Comment,
The Doctrine of Family Integrity: Protecting the
Parental Rights of Unwed Fathers Who have
Substantial Relationships With Their Children.
13 Conn. L. Rev. 145 (1980)

Article III
Of The Legislative Department

Foy and Moskowitz,
Connecticut Labor Relations Law: Recent
Developments in an Evolving Identity.
17 Conn. L. Rev. 249 (1985)

Comment,
Arbitration in Connecticut: Issues in Judicial
Intervention Under the Connecticut Arbitration
Statutes.
17 Conn. L. Rev. 387 (1985)

Article V
Of The Judicial Department

Comment,
Sticks and Stones in Connecticut Criminal Courts:
State v. Couture.
18 Conn. L. Rev. 407 (1986)

Comment,
Arbitration in Connecticut: Issues in Judicial
Intervention Under the Connecticut Arbitration
Statutes.
17 Conn. L. Rev. 387 (1985)

Comment,
Connecticut's Lis Pendens Shapes Up: Williams v.
Bartlett.
16 Conn. L. Rev. 413 (1984)

Comment,
Board of Education v. Rowley: Landmark Roadblock
or Another Signpost on the Road to State Courts.
16 Conn. L. Rev. 149 (1983)

Comment,
Court Rule-Making in Connecticut Revisited--Three
Recent Decisions: State v. King, Steadwell v.
Warden and State v. Canady.
16 Conn. L. Rev. 121 (1983)

Article VII
Of Religion

Garvey,
Free Exercise and the Values of Religious Liberty.
18 Conn. L. Rev. 779 (1986)

Tushnet,
The Constitution of Religion.
18 Conn. L. Rev. 701 (1986)

Comment,
Equal Employment of Excessive Entanglement?   The
Application of Employment Discrimination Statutes
to Religiously Affiliated Organizations.
18 Conn. L. Rev. 581 (1986)

Bleich,
Jewish   Divorce: Judicial   Misconceptions   and
Possible Means of Civil Enforcement.
16 Conn. L. Rev. 201 (1984)

Comment,
The   Role   of   Church   and   State   in   Determining
Religious   Purposes: Holy   Spirit   for   the   Unification
of World Christianity v. Tax Commissioner.
16 Conn. L. Rev. 71 (1983)

Article VIII
Of Education

Stoppleworth,
Mooney   &   Aronson   Revisited: A   Less   Than
Solomon-Like   Solution   to   the   Problem   of   Residential
Placement of Handicapped Children.
15 Conn. L. Rev. 757 (1983)

Comment,
Board of Education v. Rowley: Landmark Roadblock
or Another Signpost on the Road to State Courts.
16 Conn. L. Rev. 149 (1983)

Comment,
Employee   Right   to   Active   Union   Representation   at
Investigative   Interviews: The   Connecticut   State
Labor   Board   Decision   in   State   Department   of
Education.
16 Conn. L. Rev. 179 (1983)

Mooney and Aronson,
Solomon   Revisited: Separating   Education   and   Other
Than   Educational   Needs   in   Special   Education
Residential Placements.
14 Conn. L. Rev. 531 (1982)

Startk,
Tragic Choices in Special Education: The Effect of
Scarce Resources on the Implementation of Pub. L.
No. 94-142.
14 Conn. L. Rev. 477 (1982)

Comment,
The "Right" to Habilitation: Pennhurst State School
& Hospital v. Halderman and Youngberg v. Romeo.
14 Conn. L. Rev. 557 (1982)

Article X
Of Home Rule

Comment,
Inclusionary Zoning: An Alternative For
Connecticut Municipalities.
14 Conn. L. Rev. 789 (1982)

Comment,
The Official Responsibility Rule and Its Implications
for Municipal Liability in Connecticut.
15 Conn. L. Rev. 641 (1982)

DELAWARE

Chapter Eight
DELAWARE CONSTITUTION - 1897

Article I
Bill of Rights

Neuberger,
Separation of Church and State: Historical Roots
and Modern Interpretations.
4 Del. Law. 36 (No. 4, 1986)

Ferrara,
The New DUI Law: It's Violation of Your Rights
Will Drive You To Drink.
3 Del. Law. 58 (No. 2, 1984)

Herlihy,
The Impetus of a Tragedy: Living Wills and the
Right to Die.
2 Del. Law. 34 (No. 1, 1983)

Poole and James,
Recent   Developments   in   Delaware   Constitutional
Law.
2 Del. Law. 12 (No. 1, 1983)

Article II
Legislature

Langdon,
An Overview of Water Pollution Law.
2 Del. Law. 34 (No. 2, 1983)

Article IV
Judiciary

Schwartz,
The Delaware Chancery Court: A National Court of
Corporate Law.
2 Conn. Law. 54 (No. 3, 1984)

Article VIII
Revenue and Taxation

Gordon and Popper,
The 1985 Revisions to the Delaware Inheritance Tax
Statute.
4 Del. Law. 32 (No. 3, 1985)

Johnson,
Those "Golden Parachute" Agreements: The Taxman
Cuts the Ripcord.
10 Del. J. Corp. L. 45 (1985)

Article IX
Corporations

Hamilton,
The State of State Corporation Law: 1986.
11 Del. J. Corp. L. 1 (1986)

Siedel,
Close Corporation Law: Michigan, Delaware and the
Model Act.
11 Del. J. Corp. L. 383 (1986)

Pease,
Aronson v. Lewis: When Demand is Excused and
Delaware's Business Judgment Rule.
9 Del. J. Corp. L. 39 (1984)

Schwartz,
The Delaware Chancery Court: A National Court of
Corporate Law.
2 Conn. Law. 54 (No. 3, 1984)

Terrell,
Bricks For the Business Judgment Citadel: Recent
Developments in Delaware Corporation Law.
9 Del. J. Corp. L. 329 (1984)

Kirk,
An Overview of the Delaware Antitrust Act.
8 Del. J. Corp. L. 243 (1983)

Ferrara and Steinberg,
The Interplay Between State Corporation and
Federal Securities Law - Santa Fe, Singer, Burks,
Maldonado, Their Progeny & Beyond.
7 Del. J. Corp. L. 1 (1982)

Terrell and Nolen,
Recent Developments in Delaware Corporate Law.
7 Del. J. Corp. L. 407 (1982)

Comment,
Zapata Corp. v. Maldonado: A Limitation on the
use of Delaware's Business Judgment Rule in
Stockholder Derivative Suits.
6 Del. J. Corp. L. 80 (1981)

FLORIDA

Chapter Nine
FLORIDA CONSTITUTION - 1968

Article I
Declaration of Rights

Riggs,
Regulation of Indecency on Cable Television.
59 Fla. B.J. 9 (1985)

Ayoub,
State Action Doctrine in State and Federal Courts.
11 Fla. St. U.L. Rev. 893 (1984)

Harper,
Effective Assistance of Counsel.
58 Fla. B.J. 58 (1984)

Hering,
Nonsupport Contempt Hearing.
12 Fla. St. U.L. Rev. 117 (1984)

Hirsch,
Confidential Informants.
39 U. Miami L. Rev. 131 (1984)

Lilly,
Confrontation Clause and Ohio v. Roberts.
36 U. Fla L. Rev. 207 (1984)

Comment,
Functional Literacy Testing.
13 Stetson L. Rev. 387 (1984)

Comment,
Refusal to Take a Blood-Alcohol Test:
Constitutional Law - Self-Incrimination - Caution!
Refusal...May Be Hazardous To Your Trial.
12 Fla. St. U.L. Rev. 167 (1984)

Comment,
Jury Trial for Petty Offenses.
14 Stetson L. Rev. 191 (1984)

Comment,
Shrinking of the Fourth Amendment Umbrella.
9 Nova L.J. 231 (1984)

Comment,
Supreme Court's Treatment of Open Fields.
12 Fla. St. U.L. Rev. 637 (1984)

Comment,
Jurisprudential   Confusion   in   Eight   Amendment
Analysis.
38 U. Miami L. Rev. 357 (1984)

Comment,
Totality   of   the   Circumstances   in   Determining
Probable   Cause   for   a   Search   Warrant   Based   on
Informant's Tip.
36 U. Fla. L. Rev. 325 (1984)

Brady,
Good Faith Exception to the Exclusionary Rule.
57 Fla. B.J. 105 (1983)

Bricklemyer,
Florida Test for Taking.
57 Fla. B.J. 87 (1983)

Brown,
Defamation Law and the First Amendment.
11 Fla. St. U.L. Rev. 197 (1983)

Cohen,
Public   Employees   and   the   Privilege   Against   Self-
Incrimination.
57 Fla. B.J. 711 (1983)

Dobson,
Florida's New "Drunk Driving" Laws.
7 Nova L.J. 179 (1983)

Gunn,
Recent   Developments   in   Florida's   Guarantee   of
Access to its Courts.
57 Fla. B.J. 603 (1983)

Litchford,
Privilege Against Self-Incrimination in Civil
Litigation.
57 Fla. B.J. 139 (1983)

May,
Use of Post-Arrest Silence for Impeachment.
57 Fla. B.J. 250 (1983)

Williams,
Dissecting a Decade of Change in Florida in Forma
Pauperis Law.
12 Stetson L. Rev. 363 (1983)

Comment,
Constitutional Law: The Eighth Amendment
Requires a Determination of Actual Personal Intent
for the Death Penalty to be Imposed on Non-
Triggermen Felony Murderers.
35 U. Fla. L. Rev. 521 (1983)

Comment,
Insurance: Does Florida's No-Fault Law Comply
with the Constitutional Right of Access to the
Courts?
35 U. Fla. L. Rev. 194 (1983)

Comment,
Sufficiency-Weight Distinction.
38 U. Miami L. Rev. 147 (1983)

Comment,
Criminal Law: New Loophole in the Right to
Speedy Trial.
12 Stetson L. Rev. 494 (1983)

Comment,
Constitutional law - Search and Seizure, Pruning
the Poisonous Tree.
11 Fla. St. U.L. Rev. 451 (1983)

Fennelly,
Emergency Doctrine in Florida.
56 Fla. B.J. 873 (1982)

Jacob and Sharma,
Disciplinary and Punitive Transfer Decisions and
Due Process Values.
12 Stetson L. Rev. 1 (1982)

King,
Constitutionality of No Fault Jurisprudence.
4 Utah L. Rev. 797 (1982)

Munroe,
Consensual Electronic Surveillance.
56 Fla. B.J. 355 (1982)

Roth,
Closing the Courthouse Door.
11 Stetson L. Rev. 283 (1982)

Spence,
Voir Dire: Guaranteed Right to a Fair and
Impartial Jury.
56 Fla. B.J. 304 (1982)

Spence and Roth,
Closing the Courthouse Door.
11 Stetson L. Rev. 283 (1982)

Comment,
Criminal Law and the "Plain View Doctrine."
10 Fla. St. U.L. Rev. 290 (1982)

Comment,
Use of Contempt of Court to Enforce Florida
Divorce Decrees.
6 Nova L.J. 313 (1982)

Comment,
Automobile Exception and Search Incident to
Arrest.
11 Stetson L. Rev. 485 (1982)

Comment,
Criminal Law: It's Tough and Go at the Border.
11 Stetson L. Rev. 551 (1982)

Comment,
Automobile Exception and Search Incident to
Arrest.
11 Stetson L. Rev. 485 (1982)

Comment,
Criminal Law: It's Tough and Go at the Border.
11 Stetson L. Rev. 551 (1982)

Comment,
United States v. Ross and the Container Cases-
Another Chapter in the Police Manual On Search
and Seizure.
10 Fla. St. U.L. Rev. 471 (1982)

Carson,
What Public Employers Should Know from Hiring
Discrimination.
55 Fla. B.J. 723 (1981)

Cope,
A Quick Look at Florida's New Right of Privacy.
55 Fla. B.J. 469 (1981)

DeFoor,
Criminal Defendant's Right to participate as Co-
Counsel at Trial.
10 Stetson L. Rev. 191 (1981)

Huerta,
When does the Prosecutor's Closing Argument
Become a Comment upon the Defendant's Right to
Remain Silent?
55 Fla. B.J. 751 (1981)

Rahdert and Snyder,
Common Law Defenses to Libel and Slander.
11 Stetson L. Rev. 1 (1981)

Comment,
Warrant Requirement for Container Searches and the
"Well-Delineated" Exceptions.
36 U. Miami L. Rev. 115 (1981)

Comment,
Criminal Law: I Hear You Knocking But You Can't
Come In - Home Arrest Warrant Requirement.
10 Stetson L. Rev. 343 (1981)

Comment,
Equal Protection and Spousal Debt.
11 Stetson L. Rev. 173 (1981)

Comment,
Drug Trafficking at Airports - Judicial Response.
36 U. Miami L. Rev. 91 (1981)

Baker,
Press Rights and Government Power to Structure
the Press.
34 U. Miami L. Rev. 819 (1980)

Barett,
Securing Access by the Press and the Public to
Proceedings in Criminal Cases.
34 U. Miami L. Rev. 927 (1980)

Boyd and Lehrman,
Trials Held Behind Closed Doors.
5 Nova L.J. 1 (1980)

Marks,
Personal Right to Exclusion--A Criticism of United
States v. Calandra.
9 Stetson L. Rev. 309 (1980)

McLane,
Denial of Bail to Drug Felons.
5 Nova L.J. 81 (1980)

Oakes,
Right to Strike the Jury Trial Demand in Complex
Litigation.
34 U. Miami L. Rev. 243 (1980)

Schmidt,
Suggested Florida Constitutional Provisions Relating
to the Mentally Disabled.
54 Fla. B.J. 473 (1980)

Stotzky,
Special Privilege for the Press?
34 U. Miami L. Rev. 785 (1980)

Williams,
Right to Strike for Public Employees:
Constitutional Right to Collectively Bargain.
7 Fla. St. U.L. Rev. 475 (1980)

Winick,
Competence to Stand Trial in Florida.
35 U. Miami L. Rev. 31 (1980)

Comment,
Free Exercise of Religion.
32 U. Fla. L. Rev. 581 (1980)

Comment,
Religious Freedom: Weeding out the Coptic Church.
10 Stetson L. Rev. 138 (1980)

Comment,
Right to Die Under Florida Law.
8 Fla. St. U.L. Rev. 111 (1980)

Comment,
Prisoner's Rights: Due Process and Transfers to Mental Institutions.
32 U. Fla. L. Rev. 770 (1980)

Comment,
Criminal Law: Drug Courier Profiles.
5 Nova L.J. 141 (1980)

Comment,
Criminal Law: Exclusionary Rule.
5 Nova L.J. 131 (1980)

Comment,
Florida Exclusionary Rule Fills the Fourth Amendment--Empty Promise.
9 Stetson L. Rev. 424 (1980)

Comment,
Invocation and Waiver of Fifth Amendment Rights by Juveniles.
32 U. Fla. L. Rev. 356 (1980)

Comment,
The Elected Official's Limited Right to Financial Privacy.
15 New Eng. L. Rev. 182 (1980)

Article II
General Provisions

Belmont,
Public Interest Access to Agencies.
11 Stetson L. Rev. 454 (1982)

Comment,
Delimitation of the Maritime Boundary Between the
United States and the Bahamas.
33 U. Fla. L. Rev. 207 (1981)

Martin,
Legislative   Delegations   of   Power   and   Judicial
Review: Preventing Judicial Impotence.
8 Fla. St. U.L. Rev. 43 (1980)

Article V
Judiciary

Scheb,
Florida's   Courts   of   Appeal: Intermediate   Courts
Become Final.
13 Stetson L. Rev. 479 (1984)

Gunn,
Recent   Developments   in   Florida's   Guarantee   of
Access to its Courts.
57 Fla. B.J. 603 (1983)

Buel,
Conflict Review in the Supreme Court of a District
Court of Appeal Per Curiam Decision.
56 Fla. B.J. 849 (1982)

Mann,
Scope of the all Writs Power.
10 Fla. St. U.L. Rev. 197 (1982)

England,
Florida Appellate Reform One Year Later.
9 Fla. St. U.L. Rev. 221 (1981)

Parness,
Legislative   Roles   in   Florida's   Judicial   Rule-Making.
Jeffrey v. Parness.
33 U. Fla. L. Rev. 359 (1981)

Pratt,
Florida Supreme Court Jurisdiction - supreme Court
Jurisdiction Revisited: A Look at Five Recent
Cases.
9 Fla. St. U.L. Rev. 693 (1981)

Borgognoni,
Filing Briefs on Jurisdiction in the Supreme Court
of Florida.
54 Fla. B.J. 510 (1980)

England,
Analysis of the 1980 Jurisdictional Amendment to
Const. Art. 5 Section 3.
54 Fla. B.J. 406 (1980)

England,
Constitutional Jurisdiction of the Supreme Court of
Florida: 1980 Reform.
32 U. Fla. L. Rev. 147 (1980)

England,
In Defense of Regulation of Admission and
Discipline of Attorneys by the Supreme Court.
54 Fla. B.J. 254 (1980)

Means,
Power to Regulate Practice and Procedure in
Florida Courts.
54 Fla. B.J. 276 (1980)

Overton,
District Courts of Appeal: Courts of Final
Jurisdiction with Two New Responsibilities.
35 U. Fla. L. Rev. 80 (1980)

Article VII
Finance and Taxation

Ide,
Financing Florida's Future: Revenue Bond Law in
Florida.
12 Fla. St. U.L. Rev. 701 (1985)

Eddy,
Referendum Requirement: Constitutional Limitation on Local Government Debt in Florida.
38 U. Miami L. Rev. 677 (1984)

Hudson,
Property Appraisers.
3 Nova L.J. 477 (1983)

Comment,
Industrial Development Bonds: The Demise of the Public Purpose Doctrine.
35 U. Fla. U.L. Rev. 541 (1983)

Comment,
Counties: Supreme Court's Substantial Impact of Ad Valorem Taxation.
35 U. Fla. U.L. Rev. 175 (1983)

Miller,
Estoppel and the Public Purse.
9 Fla. St. U.L. Rev. 33 (1981)

Harria,
Allocation and Apportionment of Unitary Business Income in Florida.
8 Fla. St. U.L. Rev. 21 (1980)

Article VIII
Local Government

Coffey,
Antitrust Threat to Florida Home Rule.
56 Fla. B.J. 895 (1982)

Deal,
Constitutional Home Rule of Unchartered Counties.
56 Fla. B.J. 469 (1982)

Juergensmeyer,
Impact Fees.
9 Fla. St. U.L. Rev. 415 (1981)

Comment,
Charter County Government in Florida.
33 U. Fla. U.L. Rev. 505 (1981)

Comment,
Toward Solving The Double Taxation Dilemma
Among Florida's Local Governments.
8 Fla. St. U.L. Rev. 749 (1980)

Article IX
Education

Hudson,
Special Taxing Districts.
10 Fla. St. U.L. Rev. 49 (1982)

Article X
Miscellaneous

Williamson,
Florida Exemption Laws--Haven for Debtors or
Protection from Destitution?
15 Stetson L. Rev. 437 (1986)

Keechl,
Is there a Lottery in Florida's Future?
13 Fla. St. U.L. Rev. 901 (1985)

Mann and Jackson,
Environmental Protection Through Constitutional
Amendment.
1 J. Land Use & Envtl. L. 385 (1985)

Mattson,
Natural Resources Damages: Restitution as a
Mechanism to Slow Destruction of Florida's Natural
Resources.
1 J. Land Use & Envtl. L. 295 (1985)

Comment,
Florida's Homestead Exemption - Proceeds from the
Voluntary Sale of a Homestead.
12 Fla. St. U.L. Rev. 923 (1985)

Bricklemyer,
Florida Test for Taking.
57 Fla. B.J. 87 (1983)

Comment,
Torts - Sovereign Immunity Trilogy: Commercial
Carrier Revisited.
10 Fla. St. U.L. Rev. 702 (1983)

Miller,
Estoppel and the Public Purse.
9 Fla. St. U.L. Rev. 33 (1981)

Schwenke,
Inverse Condemnation Law.
5 Nova L.J. 167 (1981)

Article XI
Amendments

Little,
Restricting   Legislative   Amendments   to   the
Constitution.
60 Fla. B.J. 42 (1986)

Albury,
Amendment Nine and the Initiative Process: A
Costly Trip Nowhere.
14 Stetson L. Rev. 349 (1985)

Mann,
Environmental   Protection   Through   Constitutional
Amendment.
1 J. Land Use & Envtl. L. 385 (1985)

Comment,
Amendment Nine and the Initiative Process: A
Costly Trip to Nowhere.
14 Stetson L. Rev. 349 (1985)

Schmidt,
Suggested Florida Constitutional Provisions Relating
to the Mentally Disabled.
54 Fla. B.J. 473 (1980)

GEORGIA

Chapter Ten
GEORGIA CONSTITUTION - 1983

Hunter,
Georgia and the Development of Constitutional
Principles: An Essay in Honor of the Bicentennial.
24 Ga. St. B.J. 6 (1987)

Linde,
E Pluribus -- Constitutional Theory and State
Courts.
18 Ga. L. Rev. 165 (1984)

Busbee,
An Overview of the New Georgia Constitution.
35 Mercer L. Rev. 1 (1983)

Roundtree,
Constitutional Law.
33 Mercer L. Rev. 51 (1981)

Article I
Bill of Rights

Foreman,
Real Property.
36 Mercer L. Rev. 285 (1984)

Rountree,
Constitutional Law.
36 Mercer L. Rev. 137 (1984)

Pindar,
Marketability of Titles: Effect of Texaco, Inc. v.
Short.
34 Mercer L. Rev. 1005 (1983)

Rountree,
Constitutional Law.
35 Mercer L. Rev. 73 (1983)

Martin,
Contracts.
34 Mercer L. Rev. 71 (1982)

Comment,
Jurisdiction Over Nonresidents in Georgia: Crowder
v. Ginn.
17 Ga. L. Rev. 201 (1982)

Rountree,
Constitutional Law.
33 Mercer L. Rev. 51 (1981)

Williams,
Criminal Law.
33 Mercer L. Rev. 95 (1981)

Comment,
Georgia Right Against Self-Incrimination.
15 Ga. L. Rev. 1104 (1981)

Comment,
Restrictive Covenants: A Need for Reappraisal of
the Limitations Period.
17 Ga. St. B.J. 137 (1981)

Comment,
State v. Reid: Airport Searches and the Drug
Courier Profile in Georgia.
33 Mercer L. Rev. 433 (1981)

Drolet,
Criminal Law.
32 Mercer L. Rev. 35 (1980)

Comment,
Due Process Rights of Minors and Parental
Authority in Civil Commitment Cases.
31 Mercer L. Rev. 617 (1980)

Comment,
Christmas Carols in School Assemblies May Be
Constitutional.
31 Mercer L. Rev. 627 (1980)

Article III
Legislative Branch

Meeks,
Usurpation of Corporate Opportunities: Liabilities
of the Former Officer or Director.
18 Ga. St. B.J. 150 (1982)

Sentell,
Local Government Law.
34 Mercer L. Rev. 225 (1982)

Sentell,
The United States Supreme Court as Home Rule
Wrecker.
34 Mercer L. Rev. 363 (1982)

Stern,
Enforceability   of   Restrictive   Covenants   in
Employment Contracts.
17 Ga. St. B.J. 110 (1981)

Comment,
Administrative Law - Delegation of Legislative
Authority - Professional Licensure.
29 Emory L.J. 1183 (1980)

Comment,
Workers' Compensation in Georgia Municipal Law.
15 Ga. L. Rev. 57 (1980)

Article V
Executive Branch

Meals,
Legislative Delegation of Executive Power of
Appointment to Private Organizations Held
Unconstitutional.
16 Ga. St. B.J. 129 (1980)

Article VI
Judicial Branch

Busbee,
An Overview of the New Georgia Constitution.
35 Mercer L. Rev. 1 (1983)

Ellington,
Trial Practice and Procedure.
35 Mercer L. Rev. 315 (1983)

Kendrick,
Recent Developments: A Brief Survey of Recent
Developments in Georgia Juvenile Law.
34 Mercer L. Rev. 395 (1982)

Rehberg,
Wills, Trusts, and Administration of Estates.
34 Mercer L. Rev. 323 (1982)

Comment,
Jurisdiction Over Nonresidents in Georgia: Crowder
v. Ginn.
17 Ga. L. Rev. 201 (1982)

Sentell,
Local Government Law.
33 Mercer L. Rev. 187 (1981)

Williams,
Criminal Law.
33 Mercer L. Rev. 95 (1981)

Article VII
Taxation and Finance

Busbee,
An Overview of the New Georgia Constitution.
35 Mercer L. Rev. 1 (1983)

Kendrick,
Recent Developments: A Brief Survey of Recent
Developments in Georgia State and Local Taxation.
34 Mercer L. Rev. 400 (1982)

Sentell,
The County Spending Power: An Abbreviated Audit
of the Account.
16 Ga. L. Rev. 599 (1982)

Pindar,
Real Property Law.
33 Mercer L. Rev. 219 (1981)

Article VIII
Education

Busbee,
An Overview of the New Georgia Constitution.
35 Mercer L. Rev. 1 (1983)

Article IX
Counties and Municipal Corporations

Busbee,
An Overview of the New Georgia Constitution.
35 Mercer L. Rev. 1 (1983)

Sentell,
The County Spending Power: An Abbreviated Audit
of the Account.
16 Ga. L. Rev. 599 (1982)

Sentell,
Local Government Law.
34 Mercer L. Rev. 225 (1982)

Sentell,
The United States Supreme Court as Home Rule
Wrecker.
34 Mercer L. Rev. 363 (1982)

Pindar,
Real Property Law.
33 Mercer L. Rev. 219 (1981)

Poe,
Tax-Exempt Financing in Georgia.
18 Ga. St. B.J. 20 (1981)

Comment,
Workers' Compensation In Georgia Municipal Law.
15 Ga. L. Rev. 57 (1980)

Article X
Amendments to the Constitution

Monacell,
<u>Lapse or Continuation of Local Constitutional Amendments Under the Constitution of 1983</u>.
21 Ga. St. B.J. 78 (1984)

Busbee,
<u>An Overview of the New Georgia Constitution</u>.
35 Mercer L. Rev. 1 (1983)

HAWAII

Chapter Eleven
HAWAII CONSTITUTION - 1959

Article I
Bill of Rights

Comment,
State v. O'Brien: Right to Jury Trial for Driving
Under the Influence of Intoxicating Liquor.
8 U. Haw. L. Rev. 209 (1986)

Ikenaga,
Electronic Eavesdropping: Which Conversations are
Protected   from   Interception?--State   v.   Okubo,
State v. Lee.
7 U. Haw. L. Rev. 227 (1985)

Tom,
Development of Rights in Hawaii.
6 U. Haw. L.Rev. 437 (1984)

Comment,
Metromedia,   Inc.   v.   City   of   San   Diego: The
Conflict   Between   Aesthetic   Zoning   and   Commercial
Speech   Protection;   Hawaii's   Billboard   law   Under
Fire.
5 U. Haw. L. Rev. 79 (1983)

Broder,
Hawaii's Equal Rights Amendment: Its Impact On
Athletic Opportunities and Competition For Women.
2 U. Haw. L. Rev. 97 (1979)

Article III
The Legislature

Cane and Taussig,
Hawaii's 1985 Corporate Take-over Legislation: Is
It Constitutional?
8 U. Haw. L. Rev. 391 (1986)

Comment,
Development Agreement Legislation in Hawaii: An
Answer to the Vested Rights Uncertainty.
7 U. Haw. L. Rev. 173 (1985)

Comment,
Enabling and Implementing Legislation and State
Constitutional Convention Committee Reports.
6 U. Haw. L. Rev. 523 (1984)

Article VI
The Judiciary

Yoshii,
Appellate Standard of Review in hawaii.
7 U. Haw. L. Rev. 273 (1985)

Comment,
Outdoor Circle v. Harold K.L. Castle Trust Estate:
Judicial Review of Administrative Decisions.
7 U. Haw. L. Rev. 473 (1985)

Bowman,
Legitimacy and Scope of Trust Territory High Court
Power to Review Decisions of Federated States of
Micronesia Supreme Court: The Otokichy Cases.
5 U. Haw. L. Rev. 57 (1983)

Comment,
Jurisdiction: The Beginnings of the Federated
States of Micronesia Supreme Court.
5 U. Haw. L. Rev. 361 (1983)

Chang,
The Role of the State Courts After the Model
Business Corporation Act.
3 U. Haw. L. Rev. 171 (1981)

Richardson,
Judicial Independence: The Hawaii Experience.
2 U. Haw. L. Rev. 1 (1979)

Article VII
Taxation and Finance

Comment,
The Constitutionality of the Hawaii Liquor Tax
Statute: Bacchus Imports Ltd. v. Dias.
7 U. Haw. L. Rev. 387 (1985)

Comment,
Taxation: Deductibility of Business Meals - Moss
v. Commissioner of Internal Revenue.
6 U. Haw. L. Rev. 361 (1984)

Article VIII
Local Government

Comment,
The Erosion of Home Rule in Hawaii: City and
County of Honolulu v. Ariyoshi.
7 U. Haw. L. Rev. 503 (1985)

Goodin,
The Honolulu Development Plans: An Analysis of
Land Use Implications for Oahu.
6 U. Haw. L. Rev. 33 (1984)

Comment,
Resolving a Conflict: Ohana Zoning and Private
Concerns.
6 U. Haw. L. Rev. 177 (1984)

Lee and Herman,
Ensuring the Right to Equal Representation: How
to   Prepare   or   Challenge   Legislative
Reapportionment Plans.
5 U. Haw. L. Rev. 1 (1983)

Article IX
Public Health and Welfare

Comment,
Metromedia, Inc. v. City of San Diego: The
Conflict Between Aesthetic Zoning and Commercial
Speech Protection; Hawaii's Billboard Law Under
Fire.
5 U. Haw. L. Rev. 79 (1983)

Article X
Education

Comment,
Post-Majority Educational Support: Is There An
Equal Protection Violation?
6 U. Haw. L. Rev. 225 (1984)

Article XI
Conservation, Control and Development of Resources

Callies,
Regulating Paradise: Is Land Use a Right or a
Privilege?
7 U. Haw. L. Rev. 13 (1985)

Kindt and Wintheiser,
The Conservation and Protection of Marine
Mammals.
7 U. Haw. L. Rev. 301 (1985)

Goodin,
The Honolulu Development Plans: An Analysis of
Land Use Implications for Oahu.
6 U. Haw. L. Rev. 33 (1984)

Keith,
Laws Affecting the Development of Ocean Resources
in Hawaii.
4 U. Haw. L. Rev. 227 (1982)

Comment,
State-Federal Jurisdictional Conflict Over the
Internal Waters and Submerged Lands of the
Northwestern Hawaiian Islands.
4 U. Haw. L. Rev. 139 (1982)

Van Dyke and Heftel,
Tuna Management in the Pacific: An Analysis of
the South Pacific Forum Fisheries Agency.
3 U. Haw. L. Rev. 1 (1981)

Comment,
Hawaii's Ceded Lands.
3 U. Haw. L. Rev. 101 (1981)

Article XII
Hawaiian Affairs

Dannenberg,
The Office of Hawaiian Affairs and the Issue of
Sovreign Immunity.
7 U. Haw. L. Rev. 95 (1985)

Dyke,
The Constitutionality of the Office of Hawaiian
Affairs.
7 U. Haw. L. Rev. 63 (1985)

Keith,
The Hawaii State Plan Revisited.
7 U. Haw. L. Rev. 29 (1985)

IDAHO

Chapter Twelve

IDAHO CONSTITUTION - 1890

Article I
Declaration of Rights

Comment,
Racial and Religious Harassment: Idaho's Response
to a Growing Problem.
21 Idaho L. Rev. 85 (1985)

Macdonald,
Report on Civil Rights at the Idaho Youth Services
Center.
20 Idaho L. Rev. 767 (1984)

McCabe,
Haste Makes Waste: The 1983 Revision of Idaho's
DUI Statutes and Misdemeanor Criminal Rules.
20 Idaho L. Rev. 243 (1984)

Westendorf and Westenforf,
The Prouse Dicta: From Random Stops to Sobriety
Checkpoints?
20 Idaho L. Rev. 127 (1984)

Colson,
The Guarantees Idaho Farmers and Ranchers Get on
the Goods They Buy.
18 Idaho L. Rev. 177 (1982)

Comment,
Who Shall Live and Who Shall Die?: State v.
Osborn and the Idaho Death Penalty.
18 Idaho L. Rev. 195 (1982)

Comment,
Procedural Due Process Rights for Idaho Public
School Teachers: Bowler v. Board of Trustees of
School District No. 392.
17 Idaho L. Rev. 271 (1981)

Comment,
Pedigo v. Rowley: Parental Immunity in Idaho.
17 Idaho L. Rev. 301 (1981)

Kramer and Schnebeck,
Punitive Damages in Idaho.
17 Idaho L. Rev. 87 (1980)

Article III
Legislative Department

Hafen,
1986 Survey of Legislative Changes.
23 Idaho L. Rev. 137 (1987)

Krogh-Hampe,
The 1986 Idaho Water Rights Adjudication Statute.
23 Idaho L. Rev. 1 (1987)

Young,
1985 Survey of Legislative Changes.
22 Idaho L. Rev. 159 (1986)

McDevitt,
1984 Survey of Legislative Changes.
21 Idaho L. Rev. 165 (1985)

Baird,
Mineral Severance Taxes in Idaho: Considerations
for the Legislature.
19 Idaho L. Rev. 607 (1983)

Langfield,
1982 Legislative Changes.
19 Idaho L. Rev. 369 (1983)

Article V
Judicial Department

Hohnhorst,
Sixteen Years Before the Mast: The Idaho Supreme
Court and the UCC Warranties.
20 Idaho L. Rev. 1 (1984)

Gilmore,
Internal Appellate Procedure of the Supreme Court
of Idaho: A Call for Reform.
19 Idaho L. Rev. 47 (1983)

Comment,
Ruling on the New Trial Motion: What Standard for
the Idaho Trial Judge?
17 Idaho L. Rev. 249 (1981)

Article VII
Finance and Revenue

Rowland and Vache,
Taxing a Moving Target: Idaho's Income Tax Laws
as Applied to Nonresident Railroad Employees.
22 Idaho L. Rev. 343 (1986)

Baird,
Mineral Severance Taxes in Idaho: Considerations
for the Legislature.
19 Idaho L. Rev. 607 (1983)

Article VIII
Public Indebtedness and Subsidies

Moore,
Constitutional   Debt   Limitations   on   Local
Government in Idaho - Article 8, Section 3, Idaho
Constitution.
17 Idaho L. Rev. 55 (1980)

Article IX
Education and School Lands

Comment,
Procedural   Due   Process   Rights   for   Idaho   Public
School Teachers: Bowler v. Board of Trustees of
School District No. 392.
17 Idaho L. Rev. 271 (1981)

Article XV
Water Rights

Krogh-Hampe,
The 1986 Idaho Water Rights Adjudication Statute.
23 Idaho L. Rev. 1 (1987)

Schapiro,
An Argument for the Marketability of Indian
Reserved Water Rights: Tapping the Untapped
Reservoir.
23 Idaho L. Rev. 277 (1987)

Chaney,
The Last Salmon Ceremony: Implementing the
Columbia River Basin Fish and Wildlife Program.
22 Idaho L. Rev. 561 (1986)

Hockberger,
Indiscreet Regulation of Indiscrete Sources: The
Idaho Water Quality Standards and Control of
Sediment Impacts on Salmon and Steelhead Spawning
and Rearing Habitat.
22 Idaho L. Rev. 469 (1986)

Morisset,
The Legal Standards for Allocating the Fisheries
Resource.
22 Idaho L. Rev. 609 (1986)

Comment,
Fishing From the Bank: Public Recreational Rights
Along Idaho's Rivers and Lakes.
21 Idaho L. Rev. 275 (1985)

ILLINOIS

Chapter Thirteen
ILLINOIS CONSTITUTION - 1970

Article I
Bill of Rights

Hodgman and Frazer,
Withholding Life Support Treatment in Illinois--
Part I.
73 Ill. B.J. 106 (1984)

Jaffe, Aaron and Becker,
Four New Basic Sex offenses: A Fundamental Shift
in Emphasis.
72 Ill. B.J. 400 (1984)

Kling and Schwartz,
People v. Guzman: Unconstitutionality of Illinois'
Mandatory Life Imprisonment Statute.
72 Ill. B.J. 248 (1984)

Mandell,
Illinois Make a Payneful Decision.
73 Ill. B.J. 86 (1984)

Mattis,
Punitive and Compensatory Damages in Illinois
Insurance Cases: Constitutional Questions.
73 Ill. B.J. 206 (1984)

McConnell,
Blind Justice or Just Blindness?
60 Chi.-Kent L. Rev. 209 (1984)

Decker,
Collateral Consequences of a Felony Conviction in
Illinois.
56 Chi.-Kent L. Rev. 519 (1983)

Gerse,
Compensating Child's Loss of Parental Love, Care
and Affection.
1983 U. Ill. L.F. 293 (1983)

Jenkins,
Collective   Bargaining   for   Public   Employees:
Overview of Illinois' New Act.
1983 S. Ill. L.J. 483 (1983)

Linton,
Search Warrants;   Unrecorded Oral Testimony in
Support.
14 Loy. L.J. 57 (1983)

Meyering,
Court Supervision for Juvenile Delinquents.
72 Ill. B.J. 76 (1983)

Morawicz,
Sanity Examination; Fifth Amendment Rights.
72 Ill. B.J. 202 (1983)

Richter,
Conservation   Rights   in   Illinois--Meshing   Illinois
Property   Law   with   Federal   Tax   Deduction
Requirements.
71 Ill. B.J. 430 (1983)

Connor,
Employment Discrimination Law.
31 De Paul L. Rev. 323 (1982)

Grove,
Employment-At-Will.
31 De Paul L. Rev. 359 (1982)

Sampen,
Law and Equity, the Right to a Jury Trial, and
Equal Protection.
70 Ill. B.J. 376 (1982)

Scott,
Delinquency and Due Process.
59 Chi.-Kent L. Rev. 123 (1982)

Beckett,
The 1977 Illinois Death Penalty: Individualized
Focus Under the Eighth and Fourteenth Amendment.
62 Chi. B.Rec. 284 (1981)

Lane and Grossman,
Miranda: Erosion of a Doctrine.
62 Chi. B.Rec. 250 (1981)

Alexander, Lawrence and Farber,
Commercial Speech.
75 Nw. L. Rev. 307 (1980)

Decker,
Collateral Consequences of a Felony Conviction in
Illinois.
56 Chi.-Kent L. Rev. 731 (1980)

Gardner, and Ebers,
Individual Rights in Local Elections.
13 J. Marshall L. Rev. 503 (1980)

Livingston,
Open Space Preservation and Acquisition Along
Illinois Waterways.
56 Chi.-Kent L. Rev. 753 (1980)

Livingston,
Recreational Rights; Rivers and Streams.
29 De Paul L. Rev. 353 (1980)

Loverude,
Continuing Court Jurisdiction; Defendants Not
Guilty in Need of Mental Treatment.
68 Ill. B.J. 528 (1980)

Massey and Travis,
Voir Dire.
62 Chi. B.Rec. 103 (1980)

Mawdsley,
Admission of Minors to Mental Health Facilities.
69 Ill. B.J. 40 (1980)

Meites, and Flaxman,
Civil Liberties: Employment Discrimination, Due
Process, Immunities, and Exhaustion of Remedies.
56 Chi.-Kent L. Rev. 73 (1980)

Perry,
Conflict of Interest in Criminal Cases after Cuyler
v. Sullivan: Time   to   Reconsider   the   Illinois
Approach.
14 J. Marshall L. Rev. 1 (1980)

Schwartz,
A "New" Fourteenth Amendment: Decline of State
Action,   Fundamental   Rights,   and   Suspect
Classifications Under the Burger Court.
56 Chi.-Kent L. Rev. 865 (1980)

Shadur,
Advertising   and   Specialization;   Professional
Responsibility.
61 Chi. B.Rec. 324 (1980)

Singer,
Strip and Body Cavity Searches.
69 Ill. B.J. 86 (1980)

Squires, Gregory and DeWolfe,
Insurance Redlining.
29 De Paul L. Rev. 315 (1980)

Tarlock,
Administrative Law: Procedural Due Process.
56 Chi.-Kent L. Rev. 13 (1980)

Wangerin,
"Plain Error" and "Fundamental Fairness."
29 De Paul L. Rev. 753 (1980)

Widland,
Contribution: End to Active-Passive Indemnity.
69 Ill. B.J. 78 (1980)

Comment,
Breaking   the   Seal: Constitutional   and   Statutory
Approaches to Adult Adoptees' Right to Identity.
75 Nw. U.L. Rev. 316 (1980)

Comment,
Due Process for Minors "Voluntarily" Committed to
Mental Institutions.
1980 S. Ill. L.J. 171 (1980)

Article IV
The Legislature

Dillard and Martin,
Effective Dates; Laws "Passed" by the Illinois
General Assembly.
73 Ill. B.J. 434 (1985)

Leech,
Personnel Records Statute: New Rights for
Employees, New Risks for Employers.
73 Ill. B.J. 386 (1985)

Mattis,
Punitive and Compensatory Damages in Illinois
Insurance Cases: Constitutional Questions.
73 Ill. B.J. 206 (1984)

Hilliard,
Coordination of Enforcement in Environmental Law.
72 Ill. B.J. 206 (1983)

Kendall,
Regulatory Flexibility Tiering: The Law and Some
Problems.
71 Ill. B.J. 546 (1983)

Fegan,
Medical Malpractice Statute of Limitations.
70 Ill. B.J. 114 (1981)

Fins,
Law Revision Commission.
29 De Paul L. Rev. 443 (1980)

Turano,
Effective Date of New Laws--A Dangerous and
Unnecessary Hiatus.
69 Ill. B.J. 216 (1980)

Article V
The Executive

Fins,
Law Revision Commission.
29 De Paul L. Rev. 443 (1980)

Article VI
The Judiciary

Karasik,
Special Appellate Court of Workers' Compensation
Review: A Polite Proposal.
71 Ill. B.J. 44 (1982)

Mills,
Caseload Explosion: Appellate Response.
16 J. Marshall L. Rev. 1 (1982)

Cronson,
Accountability: Illinois Attorney Registration and
Disciplinary Commission.
63 Chi. B.Rec. 68 (1981)

Gulley,
Why the Illinois Attorney Registration and
Disciplinary Commission Should Not be Audited.
63 Chi. B.Rec. 78 (1981)

Mills,
Illinois Appellate Court: A Chronicle and Breviary
of Intermediate Review.
1981 S. Ill. L.J. 373 (1981)

Dahlen,
Dismissal of a Complaint or Counts Thereof.
69 Ill. B.J. 160 (1980)

Fins,
Law Revision Commission.
29 De Paul L. Rev. 443 (1980)

Article VII
Local Government

Cornfield,
Supervisory and Managerial Definitions:
Educational labor Relations Act and the Public
Labor Relations Act.
60 Chi.-Kent L. Rev. 863 (1984)

Hilliard,
Coordination of Enforcement in Environmental Law.
72 Ill. B.J. 206 (1983)

Lenahan,
Home Rule Taxation of Services.
71 Ill. B.J. 646 (1983)

Hoskins,
Municipal Antitrust Law.
70 Ill. B.J. 684 (1982)

Hall and Wallack,
Intergovernmental Cooperation and the Transfer of
Powers.
4 U. Ill. L. Rev. 775 (1981)

Comment,
Affirmative Action in Public Contracts.
30 De Paul L. Rev. 899 (1981)

Davis and Murphey,
Human Rights Act: Discrimination in Employment.
69 Ill. B.J. 218 (1980)

Hug,
Extraterritorial Powers of Illinois Municipalities
and the 1970 Illinois Constitution.
69 Ill. B.J. 32 (1980)

Livingston,
Open Space Preservation and Acquisition Along
Illinois Waterways.
56 Chi.-Kent L. Rev. 753 (1980)

Pavia,
Financing County Jail Improvements.
68 Ill. B.J. 412 (1980)

Russell,
Proposal to Repeal the Illinois Pollution Control
Board's Construction-Permit Water Regulations.
62 Chi. B.Rec. 122 (1980)

Schwartz,
Illinois School Finance--a Primer.
56 Chi.-Kent L. Rev. 831 (1980)

Comment,
A Balancing Analysis: Construction of Illinois
Home Rule Powers.
11 Loy. U. Chi. L.J. 543 (1980)

Article VIII
Finance

Cronson,
Accountability: Illinois Attorney Registration and
Disciplinary Commission.
63 Chi. B.Rec. 68 (1981)

Gulley,
Why the Illinois Attorney Registration and
Disciplinary Commission Should Not be Audited.
63 Chi. B.Rec. 78 (1981)

Article IX
Revenue

Cronson,
Accountability: Illinois Attorney Registration and
Disciplinary Commission.
63 Chi. B.Rec. 68 (1981)

Gulley,
Why the Illinois Attorney Registration and
Disciplinary Commission Should Not be Audited.
63 Chi. B.Rec. 78 (1981)

Article X
Education

Schwartz,
Illinois School Finance--A Primer.
56 Chi.-Kent L. Rev. 831 (1980)

Article XI
Environment

Hilliard,
Coordination of Enforcement in Environmental Law.
72 Ill. B.J. 206 (1983)

Comment,
Construction of Illinois Home Rule Powers.
11 Loy. U. Chi. L.J. 543 (1980)

Article XIII
General Provisions

Comment,
Cumulative Voting Rights; Elimination.
71 Ill. B.J. 502 (1983)

Decker,
Collateral Consequences of a Felony Conviction in
Illinois.
56 Chi.-Kent L. Rev. 731 (1980)

LeBlang,
Medical Negligence and the Court of Claims.
68 Ill. B.J. 534 (1980)

Palinscar,
State Employed Psychotherapists; Tort Liability.
62 Chi. B.Rec. 37 (1980)

INDIANA

Chapter Fourteen
INDIANA CONSTITUTION - 1851

Article I
Bill of Rights

Macey,
Survey of Recent Developments in Constitutional
Law.
18 Ind. L. Rev. 129 (1985)

Comment,
Ineffective Assistance of Counsel in Indiana: A
Mockery Standard.
18 Val. U.L. Rev. 481 (1984)

Johnson,
Survey of Recent Developments in Indiana Law,
Constitutional Law.
16 Ind. L. Rev. 101 (1983)

Comment,
A Maternal Duty to Protect Fetal Health?
58 Ind. L.J. 531 (1983)

Barbieri,
Survey of Recent Developments in Indiana Laws, IV.
Constitutional Law.
13 Ind. L. Rev. 89 (1980)

Falender,
Survey of Recent Developments in Indiana Law,
XIV. Property.
13 Ind. L. Rev. 343 (1980)

Mead,
Double Jeopardy Protection - Illusion or Reality?
13 Ind. L. Rev. 863 (1980)

McLemore,
Punitive Damages and Double Jeopardy: A Critical
Perspective of the Taber Rule.
56 Ind. L.J. 71 (1980)

Raphael,
Survey of Recent Developments in Indiana Law, VII.
Criminal Law and Procedure.
13 Ind. L. Rev. 187 (1980)

Comment,
Double Jeopardy and The Rule Against Punitive
Damages of Taber v. Hutson.
13 Ind. L. Rev. 999 (1980)

Article IV
Legislative

Dovenbarger,
Democracy and Distemper: An Examination of the
Sources of Judicial Distress in State Legislative
Apportionment Cases.
18 Ind. L. Rev. 885 (1985)

Article VII
Judicial

Fisher,
1983 Survey of Law on Professional Responsibility.
17 Ind. L. Rev. 283 (1984)

Jackson,
Survey of Recent Developments in Indiana Law,
XIII. Professional Responsibility and Liability.
14 Ind. L. Rev. 433 (1984)

Comment,
Exclusive Juvenile Jurisdiction to Authorize
Sterilization of Incompetent Minors.
16 Ind. L. Rev. 835 (1983)

Bubalo,
Survey of Recent Developments in Indiana Law,
XIII. Professional Responsiblity.
13 Ind. L. Rev. 325 (1980)

Article X
Finance

Boyd,
Survey of Recent Developments in Indiana Law,
Taxation.
16 Ind. L. Rev. 355 (1986)

IOWA

Chapter Fifteen
IOWA CONSTITUTION - 1857

Article I
Bill of Rights

Riley,
A Constitutional Analysis of Iowa's Bid Preference Law.
70 Iowa L. Rev. 1353 (1985)

Gangi,
Exclusionary Rule: A Case Study in Judicial Usurpation.
34 Drake L. Rev. 33 (1984-1985)

Comment,
Debt Collection Practices: Iowa Remedies for Abuse of Debtors' Rights.
68 Iowa L. Rev. 753 (1983)

Wingo,
Decisions Within the Family: A Clash of Constitutional Rights.
67 Iowa L. Rev. 401 (1982)

Comment,
Rational Basis Revised: Iowa Equal Protection after Gleason, Bierkamp, and Rudolph.
67 Iowa L. Rev. 309 (1982)

Comment,
Criminal Jury Trials In Iowa: A Time for Revision.
31 Drake L. Rev. 187 (1981-1982)

Comment,
Applicability of the Exclusionary Rule in Administrative Adjudicatory Proceedings.
66 Iowa L. Rev. 343 (1981)

Comment,
Fourth Amendment Rights of Persons Present When
a Search Warrant is Executed: Ybarra v. Illinois.
66 Iowa L. Rev. 453 (1981)

Kuhns,
Concept of Personal Aggrievement in Fourth
Amendment Standing Cases.
65 Iowa L. Rev. 493 (1980)

Vestal,
Issue Preclusion and Criminal Prosecutions.
65 Iowa L. Rev. 281 (1980)

Comment,
Equal Protection for Unmarried Parents.
65 Iowa L. Rev. 679 (1980)

Comment,
Right to the Press and Public to Attend Criminal
Trial Proceedings in Iowa.
66 Iowa L. Rev. 153 (1980)

KANSAS

Chapter Sixteen
KANSAS CONSTITUTION - 1859

Bill of Rights

Gronniger,
Juvenile Law: Juvenile Involuntarily Absent from a
Waiver Hearing is Not Denied Due Process.
25 Washburn L.J. 598 (1986)

Mark,
Practical and Constitutional Challenges to the 1985
Kansas Medical Malpractice Legislation.
25 Washburn L.J. 304 (1986)

Goering,
Constitutional Law: Privacy Penumbra Encompasses
Students in School Searches.
25 Washburn L.J. 135 (1985)

McDowell,
The Collateral Source Rule--The American Medical
Association and Tort Reform.
24 Washburn L.J. 205 (1985)

Peterson,
Home Education vs. Compulsory Attendance Laws:
Whose Kids are they Anyway?
24 Washburn L.J. 274 (1985)

Simon,
Independent But Inadequate: State Constitutions
and Protection of Freedom of Expression.
33 U. Kan. L. Rev. 305 (1985)

Kuether,
Barring the Slayer's Bounty: An Analysis of
Kansas' Troubled Experience.
23 Washburn L.J. 494 (1984)

Lundgren,
Deep Horizons--Legislative Shifting of the Burden of
Proof in Implied Covenant Cases.
24 Washburn L.J. 30 (1984)

McNeil,
The Admissibility of Child Victim Hearsay in Kansas:
A Defense Perspective.
23 Washburn L.J. 265 (1984)

Nitcher,
Criminal law: Reckless Driving Is Not a Lesser
Included Offense of Driving While Under the
Influence of Alcohol.
23 Washburn L.J. 421 (1984)

Rebein,
Criminal Procedure--Severed Defendant's Fifth
Amendment Refusal to Testify at Co-Defendant's
Trial is Admissible to Impeach Defendant's Alibi
Defense at His Own Trial--State v. Nott.
33 U. Kan. L. Rev. 189 (1984)

Roby,
Defamation: The Kansas Requirement that Private
Plaintiffs Prove Injury to Reputation Before
Recovering for Emotional harm.
23 Washburn L.J. 342 (1984)

Wright,
Constitutional Law: The Sixth Amendment Right of
Self-Representation and the Role of Standby
Counsel.
24 Washburn L.J. 164 (1984)

Gottlieb,
Reform in Kansas Domestic Violence Legislation.
31 U. Kan. L. Rev. 527 (1983)

Hanson,
Water Law--Kansas Water Appropriated Without the
Approval of the Chief Engineer.
31 U. Kan. L. Rev. 342, 349 (1983)

Pierron,
The New Kansas law Regarding Admissibility of
Child-Victim Hearsay Statements.
52 J. Kan. B.A. 88 (1983)

Spear,
Computers in the Private Sector: Right to
Informational Privacy for the Consumer.
22 Washburn L.J. 469 (1983)

Hauber,
Torts--Interspousal Immunity in Kansas: A Vestige
of a bygone Era--Guffy v. Guffy.
30 U. Kan. L. Rev. 611 (1982)

Shaiken,
Immunity From Suit on Implied Contract: Isn't It
Time Kansas Entered the 20th Century?
20 Washburn L.J. 557 (1981)

Williams,
Alien Ownership of Kansas Farmland: Can It Be
Prohibited?
20 Washburn L.J. 514 (1981)

Hageman,
Government Liability: The Kansas Tort Claims Act.
19 Washburn L.J. 260 (1980)

Kaufman,
Constitutional law: Exigent Circumstances in
Warrantless Home Arrests.
19 Washburn L.J. 345 (1980)

Martin,
Constitutional Law: Governmental Immunity Statute
Violates Equal Protection as Applied to Kansas
Turnpike Authority.
19 Washburn L.J. 581 (1980)

Article I
Executive

Little,
The New Kansas DUI Law: Constitutional Issues
and Practical Problems.
22 Washburn L.J. 340 (1983)

Article II
Legislative

McDowell,
The Collateral Source Rule--The American Medical
Association and Tort Reform.
24 Washburn L.J. (1985)

Little,
The New Kansas DUI Law: Constitutional Issues
and Practical Problems.
22 Washburn L.J. 340 (1983)

Buckner,
Rezoning in Kansas: Legislation, Adjudication, or
Confusion.
30 U. Kan. L. Rev. 571 (1982)

Hanson,
Constitutional Law - Appropriation Bills and The
Kansas One-Subject Rule--State ex rel. Stephen v.
Carlin.
30 U. Kan. L. Rev. 625 (1982)

Comment,
Treatment of the Separation of Powers Doctrine in
Kansas.
29 U. Kan. L. Rev. 243 (1981)

Hageman,
Governmental Liability: The Kansas Tort Claims
Act.
19 Washburn L.J. 260 (1980)

Article III
Judicial

Little,
The New Kansas DUI Law: Constitutional issues
and Practical Problems.
22 Washburn L.J. 340 (1983)

Article XI
Finance and Taxation

Callahan,
The Kansas Property Tax: Mischievous,
Misunderstood, and Mishandled.
22 Washburn L.J. 318 (1983)

Reece,
Urban Redevelopment: Utilization of Tax Increment
Financing.
19 Washburn L.J. 536 (1980)

Article XII
Corporations

Goetz,
The Kansas Public Employer-Employee Relations
Law.
29 U. Kan. L. Rev. 243 (1980)

Hageman,
Governmental Liability: The Kansas Tort Claims
Act.
19 Washburn L.J. 260 (1980)

Article XV
Miscellaneous

Kuether,
Barring the Slayer's Bounty: An Analysis of
Kansas' Troubled Experience.
23 Washburn L.J. 494 (1984)

Haney,
Bankruptcies in Kansas: A Need to Reform Our
Exemption Laws?
22 Washburn L.J. 286 (1983)

Pottorff,
Where Will All the Children Go: The New Kansas
Preference For Joint Custody.
32 U. Kan. L. Rev. 215 (1983)

Goetz,
The   Kansas   Public   Employer-Employee   Relations
Law.
28 U. Kan. L. Rev. 243 (1980)

KENTUCKY

Chapter Seventeen
KENTUCKY CONSTITUTION - 1891

Article I
Bill of Rights

Prygoski,
Justice Sanford and Modern Free Speech Analysis: Back to the Future?
75 Ky. L.J. 45 (1986-1987)

Comment,
The Strickland Standard for Claims of Ineffective Assistance of Counsel: Emasculating the Sixth Amendment in the Guise of Due Process.
134 U. Pa. L. Rev. 1259 (1986)

Snell,
A Plea for a Comprehensive Governmental Liability Statute.
74 Ky. L.J. 521 (1985-1986)

Comment,
Constitutional Law--Divorce Proceedings Protected Activity.
24 J. Fam. L. 710 (1985-1986)

Comment,
The Right to Independent Testing: Boon for Defendant--Burden for Prosecution?
74 Ky. L.J. 231 (1985-1986)

Comment,
The Constitutionality of Policies Requiring Strip Searches of All Misdemeanants and Minor Traffic Offenders.
54 Cin. L. Rev. 175 (1985)

Gilmer,
A Brief Look at Current Legal Writings.
46 Ky. Bench & B. 53 (1982)

Article II
Distribution of the Powers of Government

Snyder,
The Separation of Governmental Powers Under the
Constitution of Kentucky: A Legal and Historical
Analysis of L.R.C. v. Brown.
73 Ky. L.J. 165 (1984-1985)

Article III
Legislative Department

Snyder,
The Separation of Governmental Powers Under the
Constitution of Kentucky: A Legal and Historical
Analysis of L.R.C. v. Brown.
73 Ky. L.J. 165 (1984-1985)

Article X
Revenue and Taxation

Vasek,
The Impact and Desirability of Taxing Unmined Coal
Interests   in   the   Same   Manner   as   Other   Real
Property.
1 J. Min. L. & Pol'y 221 (1985-1986)

Comment,
Taxation of Unmined Minerals: Is it Inevitable, or
is it Unconstitutional.
1 J. Min. L. & Pol'y 97 (1985)

LOUISIANA

Chapter Eighteen
LOUISIANA CONSTITUTION - 1974

Article One
Declaration of Rights

Dardenne,
Can Johnny Come out and Play?--A Review of the
Constitutional Rights of the Student Athlete.
32 La. B.J. 148 (1984)

Nichols,
Entrapment and Due Process: How Far is Too Far?
58 Tul. L. Rev. 1207 (1984)

Comment,
KATZ and Dogs: Canine Sniff Inspections and the
Fourth Amendment.
44 La. L. Rev. 1093 (1984)

Comment,
Copyright and the First Amendment: Where Lies
the Public Interest?
59 Tul. L. Rev. 135 (1984)

Comment,
Supreme Court Finds First Amendment a Barrier to
Taxation of the Press.
58 Tul. L. Rev. 1073 (1984)

Comment,
Critique of Interest on Lawyers' Trust Accounts
Programs.
44 La. L. Rev. 999 (1984)

Comment,
Castration of the Male Sex Offender: A Legally
Impermissible Alternative.
30 Loy. L. Rev. (1a.) 377 (1984)

Comment,
Seizures of Personal Property Supported by
Reasonable Suspicion: United States v. Place.
44 La. L. Rev. 1149 (1984)

Baier,
Fifth Circuit Symposium: Constitutional law.
29 Loy. L. Rev. (1a.) 647 (1983)

Diamond and Cottrol,
Codifying Caste: Louisiana's Racial Classification
Scheme and the Fourteenth Amendment.
29 Loy. L. Rev. (1a.) 255 (1983)

Hargrave,
Louisiana Constitutional Law.
44 La. L. Rev. 423 (1983)

Guerriero,
Pretrial Criminal Procedure.
44 La. L. Rev. 613 (1983)

Comment,
State v. Reeves: Interpreting Louisiana's
Constitutional Right to Privacy.
44 La. L. Rev. 183 (1983)

Comment,
Survey of Recent Changes in Intestate Succession
Law Affecting Illegitimate Children--Informally
Acknowledged Child is the Ultimate Loser.
29 Loy. L. Rev. (1a.) 323 (1983)

Comment,
Pretrial Suppression Hearings: In Camera or On
Camera?
29 Loy. L. Rev. (1a.) 515 (1983)

Comment,
Comparative Analysis of the Exlusionary Rule and
Its Alternatives.
57 Tul. L. Rev. 648 (1983)

Abramovsky,
Surreptitious Recording of Witnesses in Criminal
Cases: A Quest for Truth or a Violation of Law
and Ethics?
57 Tul. L. Rev. 1 (1982)

Butler,
Constitutional and Statutory Challenges to Election
Structures: Dilution and the Value of the Right to
Vote.
42 La. L. Rev. 851 (1982)

Curry,
Constitutional Limitations on Administrative
Inspections Under the Louisiana Environmental
Affairs Ace.
29 La. B.J. 294 (1982)

Hargrave,
Louisiana Constitutional Law.
43 La. L. Rev. 505 (1982)

Hargrave,
Louisiana Constitutional Law.
42 La. L. Rev. 596 (1982)

Lamonica,
Developments in the Law, 1981-1982: Pretrial
Criminal Procedure.
43 La. L. Rev. 543 (1982)

Lines,
Scientific Creationism in the Classroom: A
Constitutional Dilemma.
28 Loy. L. Rev. (1a.) 35 (1982)

Mathias,
Exclusionary Rule Revisited.
28 Loy. L. Rev. (1a.) 1 (1982)

Murchison,
Developments in the Law, 1980-1981: Local
Government Law.
42 La. L. Rev. 564 (1982)

Pugh,
Evolving Role of Women in the Louisiana Law:
Recent Legislative and Judicial Changes.
42 La. L. Rev. 1571 (1982)

Shieber,
Electronic Surveillance, the Mafia, and Individual
Freedom.
42 La. L. Rev. 1323 (1982)

Comment,
No Habeas Corpus For the Guilty?:   Barksdale v.
Blackburn--A Time for Reappraisal.
42 La. L. Rev. 1123 (1982)

Comment,
United States v. Lee: Limitations on the Free
Exercise of Religion.
28 Loy. L. Rev. (1a.) 1216 (1982)

Comment,
Enforceability of "no damage for delay" Clauses in
Construction Contracts.
28 Loy. L. Rev. (1a.) 129 (1982)

Comment,
Appellate Review of Excessive Sentences in Non-
Capital Cases.
42 La. L. Rev. 1080 (1982)

Comment,
Proposed Federal Criminal Code and the
Government's Right to Appeal Sentences.
56 Tul. L. Rev. 693 (1982)

Comment,
Defense Witness Immunity--A "Fresh" Look at the
Compulsory Process Clause.
43 La. L. Rev. 239 (1982)

Force,
Bill of Rights and the Courts: Imperfect and
Incomplete Protection of Human Rights in Criminal
Cases.
56 Tul. L. Rev. 148 (1981)

Hargrave,
Louisiana Constitutional Law.
41 La. L. Rev. 529 (1981)

Hellerstein,
State Taxation in the Federal System: Perspectives
on Louisiana's First Use Tax on Natural Gas.
55 Tul. L. Rev. 601 (1981)

McClellan,
Fiddling with the Constitution While Rome Burns:
Case Against the Voting Rights Act of 1965.
42 La. L. Rev. 5 (1981)

Palmisano,
Quest for Justice Against Wrongful Medical
Malpractice Suit: Louisiana's Unique Advantage.
27 Loy. L. Rev. (1a.) 325 (1981)

Pugh and Radamaker,
Plea for Greater Judicial Control Over Sentencing
and Abolition of the Present Plea Bargaining
System.
42 La. L. Rev. 79 (1981)

Sullivan,
Developments in the law, 1979-1980:   Criminal Trial
Procedure.
41 La. L. Rev. 582 (1981)

Comment,
State v. Bolden: Louisiana's Anomalous Reliance on
the Anonymous Informant.
41 La. L. Rev. 719 (1981)

Comment,
Legitimate Interest Privilege and the Public
Disclosure Tort: Campbell v. Seabury Press.
41 La. L. Rev. 917 (1981)

Comment,
Louisiana's Alimony Provisions: A Move Toward
Sexual Equality.
41 La. L. Rev. 941 (1981)

Comment,
Problematic Application of Succession of Brown.
41 La. L. Rev. 1314 (1981)

Comment,
Sexual Harassment in the Workplace: New
Guidelines from the EEOC.
27 Loy. L. Rev. (1a.) 512 (1981)

Comment,
The 1978 Amendment to Title VII: Legislative
Reaction to the Gedulding-Gilbert-Satty Pregnancy
Exclusion Problem in Disability Benefits Programs.
27 Loy. L. Rev. (1a.) 532 (1981)

Comment,
Illegitimates and Louisiana Succession Law.
55 Tul. L. Rev. 585 (1981)

Comment,
In Re Grand Jury Subpoenas--Juveniles' Right to
Counsel Inside the Grand Jury.
41 La. L. Rev. 1305 (1981)

Comment,
Another Look at Louisiana Succession Law:
Ramifications of Succession of Brown.
41 La. L. Rev. 1256 (1981)

Comment,
Rhode Island v. Innis: A Heavy Blow to the Rights
of a Suspect in Custody; and No "Christian Burial"
to Ease the Passage.
41 La. L. Rev. 928 (1981)

Comment,
Civilian Thoughts on U.C.C. Section 9-503 Self-
Help Repossession: Reasoning in a Historical
Vacuum.
42 La. L. Rev. 239 (1981)

Amaker,
De Facto Leadership and the Civil Rights Movement:
Perspective on the Problems and Role of Activists
and Lawyers in Legal and Social Change.
6 S.U.L. Rev. 225 (1980)

Carleton,
Elitism Sustained: Louisiana Constitution of 1974.
54 Tul. L. Rev. 560 (1980)

Coon,
Law of Interdiction: Time for Change.
27 La. B.J. 223 (1980)

Hargrave,
Louisiana Constitutional Law.
40 La. L. Rev. 717 (1980)

Joseph,
Work of the Louisiana Appellate Courts for the
1978-1979 Term: Criminal Law and Procedure.
40 La. L. Rev. 635 (1980)

Comment,
Entering the Door Opened: An Evolution of Rights
of Public Access to Governmental Deliberations in
Louisiana and a Plea for Realistic Remedied.
41 La. L. Rev. 192 (1980)

Comment,
Davis v. Passman: A Private Cause of action for
Damages Under the Due Process Clause of the Fifth
Amendment.
41 La. L. Rev. 275 (1980)

Comment,
Implied Consent Statutes and the Requirements of
Due Process: Are they Compatible?
26 Loy. L. Rev. (1a.) 180 (1980)

Comment,
EEOC May Seek Classwide Relief Without Being
Certified as a Class Representative Under Fed.
Rules Civ. Proc. Rule 23.
55 Tul. L. Rev. 237 (1980)

Comment,
Protecting the Handicapped from Employment
Discrimination in Private Sector Employment: A
Critical Analysis of Section 503 of the Federal
Rehabilitation Ace of 1973.
54 Tul. L. Rev. 717 (1980)

Comment,
Expropriation: Compensating the Landowner to the
Full Extent of His Loss.
40 La. L. Rev. 817 (1980)

Comment,
A Private Mall Becomes a Public Hall.
26 Loy. L. Rev. (1a.) 739 (1980)

Comment,
Covert Entry, Electronic Surveillance, and the
Fourth Amendment: Dalia v. United States.
40 La. L. Rev. 95 (1980)

Comment,
Entering the Door Opened: An Evolution of Rights
of Public Access to Governmental Deliberations in
Louisiana and a Plea for Realistic Remedies.
41 La. L. Rev. 192 (1980)

Comment,
Fourth   Amendment--Automatic   Standing   for
Defendants Charged with Possessory Crimes is
Overruled.
55 Tul. L. Rev. 250 (1980)

Comment,
Rakas v. Illinois: The Fourth Amendment and
Standing Revisited.
40 La. L. Rev. 962 (1980)

Comment,
Threshold of the Fourth Amendment.
26 Loy. L. Rev. (1a.) 730 (1980)

Comment,
History and Utility of the Supreme Court's Present
Definition of Religion.
26 Loy. L. Rev. (1a.) 87 (1980)

Comment,
Right to Trial by Jury: New Guidelines for State
Criminal Trial Juries.
40 La. L. Rev. 837 (1980)

Comment,
Six-Member Juries: Unanimous Verdicts in State
Criminal Trials for Nonpetty Offenses.
54 Tul. L. Rev. 1178 (1980)

Article II
Distribution of Powers

Comment,
Critique of Interest on lawyers' Trust Accounts
Programs.
44 La. L. Rev. 999 (1984)

Forman,
Are Louisiana Judicial Death Warrants
Constitutional?
31 La. B.J. 17 (1983)

Patterson,
Discharged Counsel: Dilemma Solved?
28 La. B.J. 177 (1981)

Comment,
Judicial Review of the Legislative Enactment
Process: Louisiana's "Journal Entry" Rule.
41 La. L. Rev. 1187 (1981)

Comment,
League of Women Voters v. City of New Orleans:
Standing or Political Question?
41 La. L. Rev. 1345 (1981)

Article III
Legislative Branch

Comment,
Medical Malpractice: A Sojourn Through the
Jurisprudence Addressing Limitation of Liability.
30 Loy. L. Rev. (1a.) 119 (1984)

Hargrave,
"Statutory" and "Hortatory" Provisions of the
Louisiana Constitution of 1974.
43 La. L. Rev. 647 (1983)

Murchison,
Developments   in   the   Law,   1982-1983:   Local
Government Law.
44 La. L. Rev. 373 (1983)

Engstrom,
Post-Census Representational Districting: Supreme
Court,   "One   person,   One   Vote,"   and   the
Gerrymandering Issue.
7 S.U.L. Rev. 173 (1981)

Comment,
Judicial   Review   of   the   Legislative   Enactment
Process: Louisiana's "Journal Entry" Rule.
41 La. L. Rev. 1187 (1981)

Carleton,
Elitism Sustained: Louisiana Constitution of 1974.
54 Tul. L. Rev. 560 (1980)

Hargrave,
Work of the Louisiana Appellate Courts for the
1978-1979 Term: Louisiana Constitutional Law.
40 La. L. Rev. 717 (1980)

Yiannopoulos,
Louisiana Civil Law: A Lost Cause?
54 Tul. L. Rev. 830 (1980)

Comment,
Entering the Door Opened: An Evolution of Rights
of Public Access to Governmental Deliberations in
Louisiana and a Plea for Realistic Remedies.
41 La. L. Rev. 192 (1980)

Article IV
Executive Branch

Comment,
Constitutionality of Louisiana Aid to Private
Education.
44 La. L. Rev. 865 (1984)

Uddo,
"Who's in Charge?": Louisiana Governor's Power to
Act in Absentia.
29 Loy. L. Rev. (1a.) 1 (1983)

Comment,
Judicial Review of the Legislative Enactment
Process: Louisiana's "Journal Entry" Rule.
41 La. L. Rev. 1187 (1981)

Carleton,
Elitism Sustained: Louisiana Constitution of 1974.
54 Tul. L. Rev. 560 (1980)

Hargrave,
Work of the Louisiana Appellate Courts for the
1978-1979 Term: Louisiana Constitutional Law.
40 La. L. Rev. 717 (1980)

Murchison,
Work of the Louisiana Appellate Courts for the
1978-1979 Term: Local Government Law.
40 La. L. Rev. 681 (1980)

Comment,
Gulf States Utilities, the Public Service Commission,
and the Supreme Court: On Raising the Electric
Rates.
40 La. L. Rev. 1048 (1980)

Article V
Judicial Branch

Percy,
Should State Judges be Elected or Appointed?
31 La. B.J. 274 (1984)

Comment,
Critique of Interest of Lawyers' Trust Accounts
Programs.
44 La. L. Rev. 999 (1984)

Dixon,
Judicial Method in Interpretation of Law in
Louisiana.
42 La. L. Rev. 596 (1982)

Hargrave,
Developments in the Law, 1980-1981: Louisiana
Constitutional law.
43 La. L. Rev. 596 (1982)

Comment,
Insanity Defense in Louisiana: Presumptions, Burden
of Proof and Appellate Review.
42 La. L. Rev. 1166 (1982)

Comment,
Appellate Review of Excessive Sentences in Non-
Capital Cases.
42 La. L. Rev. 1080 (1982)

Comment,
Concept of an "Earned Fee" In the Regulation of
Attorney's Fees by Louisiana Supreme Court.
42 La. L. Rev. 1181 (1982)

Hargrave,
Developments in the law, 1981-1982: Louisiana
Constitutional Law.
41 La. L. Rev. 529 (1981)

Patterson and Hardin,
Discharged Counsel: Dilemma Solved?
28 La. B.J. 177 (1981)

Comment,
In Re Grand Jury Subpoenas--Juveniles' Right to
Counsel Inside the Grand Jury.
41 La. L. Rev. 1305 (1981)

Comment,
Appellate Review and the Lesser Included Offense
Doctrine in Louisiana.
27 Loy. L. Rev. (1a.) 284 (1981)

Comment,
League of Women Voters v. City of New Orleans:
Standing or Political Question?
41 La. L. Rev. 1345 (1981)

Dennis,
Use of Our Courts of Appeal for Speedier Criminal
Justice.
28 La. B.J. 39 (1980)

Joseph,
Criminal Law and Procedure.
40 La. L. Rev. 635 (1980)

Maraist,
Civil Procedure.
40 La. L. Rev. 751 (1980)

Tate,
"New" Judicial Solution: Occasions For and Limits
to Judicial Creativity.
54 Tul. L. Rev. 877 (1980)

Comment,
Prosecutor's Dilemma--A Duty to Disclose or a Duty
not to Commit Reversible Error.
40 La. L. Rev. 513 (1980)

Article VI
Local Government

Backstrom and Nuzum,
Where, Oh Where is the Lease Tax Due?   Lafayette
Parish School Board v. Market Leasing Co., Inc.
31 La. B.J. 346 (1984)

Hargrave,
"Statutory"   and   "Hortatory"   Provisions   of   the
Louisiana Constitution of 1974.
43 La. L. Rev. 647 (1983)

Comment,
New Orleans Fiscal Crisis: When Debt Ceilings and
Taxing Limitations Really Pinch.
55 Tul. L. Rev. 850 (1981)

Carleton,
Elitism Sustained: Louisiana Constitution of 1974.
54 Tul. L. Rev. 560 (1980)

Marcel and Bockrath,
Regional Governments and Coastal Zone Management
in Louisiana.
40 La. L. Rev. 887 (1980)

Article VII
Revenue and Finance

Edwards, Zehner and Moore,
Constitutional and Policy Implications of Louisiana's
Proposed Environmental Energy Tax: Political
Expediency or Effective Regulation?
58 Tul. L. Rev. 215 (1983)

Pierce,
Constitutionality of State Environmental Taxes.
58 Tul. L. Rev. 169 (1983)

Murchison,
Developments in the Law, 1981-1982:   Local
Government Law.
43 La. L. Rev. 461 (1982)

Comment,
New Orleans Fiscal Crisis: When Debt Ceilings and
Taxing Limitations Really Pinch.
55 Tul. L. Rev. 850 (1981)

Comment,
League of Women Voters v. City of New Orleans:
Standing or Political Question?
41 La. L. Rev. 1345 (1981)

Carleton,
Elitism Sustained.
54 Tul. L. Rev. 560 (1980)

Hargrave,
Developments in the law, 1979-1980:   Louisiana
Constitutional Law.
41 La. L. Rev. 529 (1980)

Article VIII
Education

Bouillion,
Louisiana Constitution, Article VIII: Education.
46 La. L. Rev. 1137 (1986)

Comment,
Constitutionality of Louisiana Aid to Private
Education.
44 La. L. Rev. 865 (1984)

Comment,
Legal Rights and Passage of Time.
41 La. L. Rev. 220 (1980)

Article IX
Natural Resources

Comment,
Ground Water: Louisiana's Quasi-Fictional and
Truly Fugacious Mineral.
44 La. L. Rev. 1123 (1984)

Hargrave,
"Statutory" and "Hortatory" Provisions of the
Louisiana Constitution of 1974.
43 La. L. Rev. 647 (1983)

Symeonides,
Developments in the Law, 1982-1983: Property.
44 La. L. Rev. 505 (1983)

Hargrave,
Developments in the Law, 1981-1982: Louisiana
Constitutional Law.
43 La. L. Rev. 505 (1982)

Jenkins and Hribernick,
State Taxation of Interstate Commerce: "It is a
Question of Power."
42 La. L. Rev. 951 (1982)

McCowan,
Louisiana Environmental Law and Regulations.
29 La. B.J. 171 (1981)

Wall,
Imprescriptible Mineral Interests in Louisiana.
42 La. L. Rev. 123 (1981)

Comment,
Public Trust Doctrine as a Basis for Environmental
Litigation in Louisiana.
27 Loy. L. Rev. (1a.) 469 (1981)

Article X
Public Officials and Employees

Stockstill,
Voting and Election Law in the Louisiana
Constitution.
46 La. L. Rev. 1253 (1986)

Segal,
Power to Probe into Matters of Vital Public
Importance.
58 Tul. L. Rev. 941 (1984)

Hargrave,
Louisiana Constitutional Law.
44 La. L. Rev. 423 (1983)

L'Enfant,
Louisiana Civil Procedure.
44 La. L. Rev. 411 (1983)

Force and Griffith,
Louisiana Administrative Procedure Act.
42 La. L. Rev. 1227 (1982)

Carleton,
Elitism Sustained: Louisiana Constitution of 1974.
54 Tul. L. Rev. 560 (1980)

Hargrave,
Work of the Louisiana Appellate Courts for the
1978-1979 Term: Louisiana Constitutional law.
40 La. L. Rev. 717 (1980)

Article XII
General Provisions

Comment,
Deputy Sheriff--Public officer or Public Employee?
Consequences in Light of Modern Day Workmen's
Compensation and Tort Law.
44 La. L. Rev. 1075 (1984)

Claiborne,
An Analysis of the Louisiana Constitution of 1921
and 1974, and Their Impact on Louisiana Trust Law.
10 S.U.L. Rev. 65 (1983)

Dakin,
Expropriation.
44 La. L. Rev. 357 (1983)

Hargrave,
"Statutory" and "Hortatory" Provisions of the
Louisiana Constitution of 1974.
43 La. L. Rev. 647 (1983)

Comment,
Pretrial Suppression Hearings: In Camera or On
Camera.
29 Loy. L. Rev. (1a.) 515 (1983)

LeVan,
Developments in the Law, 1980-1981: Trusts and
Estates.
42 La. L. Rev. 454 (1982)

Lorio,
Louisiana Trusts: Experience of a Civil Law
Jurisdiction with the Trust.
42 La. L. Rev. 1721 (1982)

Murchison,
Local Government Law.
42 La. L. Rev. 564 (1982)

Stone and Rinker,
Government Liability for Negligent Inspections.
57 Tul. L. Rev. 328 (1982)

Comment,
New Hope for the Survivor: Changes in the
Usufruct of the Surviving Spouse.
28 Loy. L. Rev. (1a.) 1095 (1982)

Smith,
Victims' Rights Vis-a-Vis the State.
29 La. B.J. 176 (1981)

Comment,
Illegitimates and Louisiana Succession Law.
55 Tul. L. Rev. 585 (1981)

Comment,
Another Look at Louisiana Succession Law:
Ramifications of Succession of Brown.
41 La. L. Rev. 1256 (1981)

Comment,
Entering the Door Opened: An Evolution of Rights
of Public Access to Governmental Deliberations in
Louisiana and a Plea for Realistic Remedies.
41 La. L. Rev. 192 (1980)

MAINE

Chapter Nineteen
MAINE CONSTITUTION - 1983

Article I
Declaration of Rights

Trowbridge,
Restraining the Prosecutor: Restrictions on
Threatening Prosecution for Civil Ends.
37 Me. L. Rev. 41 (1985)

Tinkle,
Resurgence of State Constitutional Law.
18 Me. B.Bull. 257 (1984)

Comment,
Maine's IOLTA Proposal: A Source of Supplemental
Funding for Legal Services.
36 Me. L. Rev. 359 (1984)

Comment,
Status of Jury Trial Waivers in Maine's District
Court.
36 Me. L. Rev. 423 (1984)

Culley,
In Defense of Civil Juries.
35 Me. L. Rev. 17 (1983)

Sheldon,
Obsolescence of Voluntary Confessions in Maine.
35 Me. L. Rev. 243 (1983)

Comment,
Constitutional Issues Raised By Civil-Criminal
Dichotomy of Maine OUI Law.
35 Me. L. Rev. 385 (1983)

Comment,
State v. Sweatt: Examination of Current Confusion
in Fourth Amendment Standing.
35 Me. L. Rev. 209 (1983)

Alexander,
Civil Juries: Are Benefits Worth Costs?
34 Me. L. Rev. 63 (1982)

Comment,
Constitutional Law of Defamation; Developments and
Suggested State Court Responses.
33 Me. L. Rev. 371 (1981)

Comment,
"Fighting Words" and First Amendment.
33 Me. L. Rev. 445 (1981)

Comment,
Development and Consequences of "Good Faith"
Exception to Exclusionary Rule and Qualified "Good
Faith" Immunity From Liability.
33 Me. L. Rev. 325 (1981)

Lobsenz,
Bakke, Lochner, and Law School: Nobility Clause
Versus a Republican Form of Medicine.
32 Me. L. Rev. 1 (1980)

Comment,
Abortion: Testing Constitutional Limits.
32 Me. L. Rev. 315 (1980)

Comment,
Role of Foreseeability in Jurisdictional Inquiry.
32 Me. L. Rev. 497 (1980)

Article IV
Part Third: Legislative Power

Hudon,
Cheaper Booze at Kittery: Is it Constitutional?
19 Me. B.Bull. 1 (1985)

MARYLAND

Chapter Twenty
MARYLAND CONSTITUTION - 1967

Declaration of Rights

Berson,
Senior Citizens: Over 60 Does Not Mean Over the Hill.
13 Current Mun. Probs. 13 (1986)

Comment,
Survey of Developments in Maryland Law, 1983-1984.
44 Md. L. Rev. 481 (1985)

Comment,
Whether Premature Verdict Rendered Before Summation, Even if Stricken, Amounts to a Denial of Right to Assistance of Counsel.
13 U. Balt. L. Rev. 383 (1984)

Bogen,
The Origins of Freedom of Speech and Press.
42 Md. L. Rev. 429 (1983)

Cancila,
"Wrongful Birth" Lawsuits Raise Complex Social Issues.
26 Am. Med. News 2 (1983)

Leviton and Shuger,
Maryland's Exchangeable Children: A Critique of Maryland's System of Providing Services to Mentally Handicapped Children.
42 Md. L. Rev. 823 (1983)

Ester,
Maryland Custody Law--Fully Committed to the Child's Best Interests.
41 Md. L. Rev. 225 (1982)

Comment,
Parent-Child Tort Immunity: Time for Maryland to
Abrogate an Anachronism.
11 U. Balt. L. Rev. 435 (1982)

Comment,
Rights of the Maryland Probationer: A Primer for
the Practitioner.
11 U. Balt. L. Rev. 272 (1982)

McLain,
The EEOC Sexual Harassment Guidelines: Welcome
Advances Under Title VII.
10 U. Balt. L. Rev. 275 (1981)

Brown,
The Law/Equity Dichotomy in Maryland.
39 Md. L. Rev. 427 (1980)

Dilloff,
Never on a Sunday: The Blue Laws Controversy.
39 Md. L. Rev. 679 (1980)

Linch,
Directed   Verdict   in   Maryland: Less   Obvious
Applications of a Simple Rule.
9 U. Balt. L. Rev. 217 (1980)

Linde,
First   Things   First: Rediscovering   the   States'   Bills
of Rights.
9 U. Balt. L. Rev. 74 (1980)

Quinn,
The   Health   Care   Malpractice   Claims   Statute:
Maryland's   Response   to   the   Medical   Malpractice
Crisis.
10 U. Balt. L. Rev. 74 (1980)

Rees,
State   Constitutional   Law   for   Maryland   Lawyers:
Judicial Relief for Violations of Rights.
10 U. Balt. L. Rev. 102 (1980)

Comment,
Felon is Culpable for Murder in the First Degree
Under Maryland's Felony-Murder Statute When
Police Officer Kills Kidnapped Hostage Used by
Felon as Human Shield.
9 U. Balt. L. Rev. 508 (1980)

Comment,
Criminal Conversation--Judicial Abrogation of the
Civil Action for Adultery.
10 U. Balt. L. Rev. 205 (1980)

Comment,
Maryland Rule 746 Requires That Criminal Charges
be Dismissed When State Fails to Bring Case to
Trial Within Prescribed Period and Fails to Establish
Extraordinary Cause Justifying Postponement.
9 U. Balt. L. Rev. 473 (1980)

Article I
Elective Franchise

Rees,
State Constitutional Law for Maryland Lawyers:
Judicial Relief for Violation of Rights.
10 U. Balt. L. Rev. 102 (1980)

Article III
Legislative Department

Comment,
Survey of Developments in Maryland Law, 1983-1984.
44 Md. L. Rev. 400 (1985)

Comment,
Eminent Domain: Private Corporations and the
Public Use Limitation.
11 U. Balt. L. Rev. 310 (1982)

Comment,
Bank Credit Card Interest Rates in Maryland: How
High Can They Go.
11 U. Balt. L. Rev. 517 (1982)

Brown,
The Law/Equity Dichotomy in Maryland.
39 Md. L. Rev. 427 (1980)

Rees,
State Constitutional Law for Maryland Lawyers:
Judicial Relief for Violation of Rights.
10 U. Balt. L. Rev. 102 (1980)

Article IV
Judiciary Department

Adams,
Application of Selected Techniques of Time-Series
Analysis to Court Caseload Data.
9 Just. Sys. J. 351 (1984)

Comment,
Maryland Jury as "Judges of Law."
1981 Det. C.L. Rev. 873 (1981)

Brown,
The Law/Equity Dichotomy in Maryland.
39 Md. L. Rev. 427 (1980)

Quinn,
The Health Care Malpractice Claims Statute:
Maryland's Response to the Medical Malpractice
Crisis.
10 U. Balt. L. Rev. 74 (1980)

Rees,
State Constitutional Law for Maryland Lawyers:
Judicial Relief for Violations of Rights.
10 U. Balt. L. Rev. 102 (1980)

Article VIII
Education

Leviton and Shuger,
Maryland's Exchangeable Children: A Critique of
Maryland's System of Providing Services to Mentally
Handicapped Children.
42 Md. L. Rev. 823 (1983)

Article XIV
Amendments to the Constitution

Comment,
Interaction and Interpretation of the Budget and
Referendum Amendments of the Maryland
Constitution.
39 Md. L. Rev. 558 (1980)

Article XVI
The Referendum

Staller,
Maryland Reform Measure Ignores Litigation
Realities.
1986 U. Pa. L.J. Rev. 3 (1986)

MASSACHUSETTS

Chapter Twenty-one
MASSACHUSETTS CONSTITUTION - 1780

Preamble

Hennessey,
The Extraordinary Massachusetts Constitution of 1780.
14 Suffolk U.L. Rev. 873 (1980)

Reid,
In The Taught Tradition: The Meaning of Law in Massachusetts Bay Two-Hundred Years Ago.
14 Suffolk U.L. Rev. 931 (1980)

Part the First
A Declaration of the Rights of the Inhabitants of the Commonwealth of Massachusetts

Cronin and Fieldsteel,
When Does Environmental Regulation of Private Property Become a Taking and Require Compensation?
70 Mass. L. Rev. 72 (1985)

Heins,
"The Marketplace and the World of ideas": A Substitute for State Action as a Limiting Principle Under the Massachusetts Equal Rights Amendment.
18 Suffolk U.L. Rev. 347 (1984)

Greenberg,
Double Jeopardy and Trial de Novo, The Dilemma in the State's District Courts.
68 Mass. L. Rev. 50 (1983)

Crane, Howard, Schmidt and Schwartz,
The Massachusetts Constitutional Amendment Prohibiting Discrimination on the Basis of Handicap: Its Meaning and Implementation.
16 Suffolk U.L. Rev. 47 (1982)

Jerison,
Home Rule in Massachusetts.
67 Mass. L. Rev. 51 (1982)

Kiely,
Warrantless Electronic Surveillance in Massachusetts.
67 Mass. L. Rev. 183 (1982)

Montgomery and Wald,
The Right to Trial by Jury in C. 93A Actions.
67 Mass. L. Rev. 79 (1982)

Reid,
Selected Bibliography Massachusetts Constitution.
14 Suffolk U.L. Rev. 931 (1980)

Wilkins,
Judicial Treatment of the Massachusetts Declaration
of Rights in Relation to Cognate Provisions of
United States Constitution.
14 Suffolk U.L. Rev. 931 (1980)

Part The Second
Frame of Government

Cella,
The People of Massachusetts, a New Republic, and
the Constitution of 1780: The Evolution of
Principles of Popular Control of Political Authority
1774-1780.
14 Suffolk U.L. Rev. 875 (1980)

Hennessey,
The Extraordinary Massachusetts Constitution of
1780.
14 Suffolk U.L. Rev. 873 (1980)

Rineer,
Selected Bibliography Massachusetts Constitution of
1780.
14 Suffolk U.L. Rev. 1107 (1980)

Chapter I
The Legislative Power

Taylor,
Lawyer John Adams and the Massachusetts
Constitution.
24 Boston B.J. 21 (1980)

Chapter II
The Executive Power

Taylor,
Lawyer John Adams and the Massachusetts
Constitution.
24 Boston B.J. 21 (1980)

Chapter III
The Judicial Power

Montgomery,
The Right to Trial by Jury in C. 93A Actions.
67 Mass. L. Rev. 79 (1982)

Taylor,
Lawyer John Adams and the Massachusetts
Constitution.
24 Boston B.J. 21 (1980)

Wilkins,
Judicial Treatment of the Massachusetts Declaration
of Rights in Relation to Cognate Provisions of the
United States Constitution.
14 Suffolk U.L. Rev. 887 (1980)

Articles of Amendment

Cronin and Fieldsteel,
When Does Environmental Regulation of Private
Property Become a Taking and Require
Compensation?
70 Mass. L. Rev. 72 (1985)

Crare, Howard, Schmidt and Schwartz,
The   Massachusetts   Constitutional   Amendment
Prohibiting Discrimination on the Basis of Handicap:
Its Meaning and Implementation.
16 Suffolk U.L. Rev. 47 (1982)

Jerison,
Home Rule in Massachusetts.
67 Mass. L. Rev. 51 (1982)

Goren,
A   New   System   of   Property   Taxation   in   the
Commonwealth.
65 Mass. L. Rev. 209 (1980)

MICHIGAN

Chapter Twenty-two
MICHIGAN CONSTITUTION - 1963

Article I
Declaration of Rights

Sadler,
Supplemental Protection of Individual Rights Under
the Michigan Constitution.
64 Mich. B.J. 102 (1985)

Comment,
Motions for Appointment of Counsel and the
Collateral Order Doctrine.
83 Mich. L. Rev. 1547 (1985)

Curtner,
Constitutional Law.
30 Wayne L. Rev. 385 (1984)

Harris,
Back to Basics: An Examination of the Exclusionary
Rule in Light of Common Sense and the Supreme
Court's Original Search and Seizure Jurisprudence.
37 Ark. L. Rev. 646 (1984)

Rubin,
When the Governed Criticize Their Govenors:
Parameters of Public Employees' Free-Speech Rights.
10 Empl. Rel. L.J. 106 (1984)

Comment,
Public Employees or Private Citizens: The Off-
Duty Sexual Activities of Police Officers and the
Constitutional Right of Privacy.
18 U. Mich. J.L. Ref. 195 (1984)

Comment,
The Attenuation Exception to the Exclusionary Rule:
A Study in Attenuated Principle and Dissipated
Logic.
75 J. Crim. L & Criminology 139 (1984)

Comment,
Self-Defense and the State's Burden of Proof Under
the Due Process Clause: State v. McCullum.
20 Willamette L. Rev. 179 (1984)

Comment,
Racially-Motivated   Violence   and   Intimidation:
Inadequate   State   Enforcement   and   Federal   Civil
Rights Remedies.
75 J. Crim. L. & Criminology 103 (1984)

Alschuler,
Implementing   the   Criminal   Defendant's   Right   to
Trial: Alternatives to the Plea Bargaining System.
50 U. Chi. L. Rev. 931 (1983)

Goodpaster,
The Trial for Life: Effective Assistance of Counsel
in Death Penalty Cases.
58 N.Y.U. L. Rev. 299 (1983)

Ison,
Fourth   Amendment--Officer   Safety   and   the
Protective Automobile Search: An Expansion of the
Pat-Down Frisk.
74 J. Crim. L. & Criminology 1265 (1983)

LaFave,
Fourth   Amendment   Vagaries   (Of   Improbable   Cause,
Imperceptible   Plain   View,   Notorious   Privacy,   and
Balancing Askew).
74 J. Crim. L. & Criminology. 1171 (1983)

Lippitt,
Running the Gauntlet of Criminal Defense.
60 U. Det. J. Urb. L. 169 (1983)

Sickman,
Fourth   Amendment--Limited   Luggage   Seizures   Valid
on Reasonable Suspicion.
74 J. Crim. L. & Criminology 1265 (1983)

Slonim,
How Effective Does a Criminal Defense Have to be?
69 A.B.A. J. 1030 (1983)

Comment,
Constitutional Law-Equal Protection-Public
Education for Undocumented Aliens--Phyler v. Doe.
29 Wayne L. Rev. 1487 (1983)

Comment,
Discriminatory Purpose and Mens Rea: The
Tortured Argument of Invidious Intent.
93 Yale L.J. 111 (1983)

Comment,
Criminal Procedure--Automobile Exception to
Warrant Requirement, United States v. Ross.
6 U. Ark. Little Rock L.J. 331 (1983)

Comment,
Is Equality a Totally Empty Idea?
81 Mich. L. Rev. 600 (1983)

Comment,
The Rights of Minors to Freedom of Religion.
62 Mich. B.J. 441 (1983)

Comment,
Content Regulation and the Dimensions of Free
Expression.
96 Harv. L. Rev. 1854 (1983)

Comment,
INS Surveys of Business Establishments:
Reasonable, Individualized Suspicion of Illegal
Alienage.
78 Nw. U.L. Rev. 632 (1983)

Comment,
Due Process, Court Access Fees, and the Right to
Litigate.
57 N.Y.U. L. Rev. 768 (1983)

Bartholet,
Application of Title VII to Jobs in High Places.
95 Harv. L. Rev. 945 (1982)

Martin,
On a New Argument for Freedom of Speech.
57 N.Y.U. L. Rev. 906 (1982)

Wells,
Affirmative Duty and Constitutional Tort.
16 U. Mich. J.L. Ref. 1 (1982)

Comment,
A Proposed Analysis for Gender-Based Practices and
State Public Accommodations Laws.
16 U. Mich. J.L. Ref. 135 (1982)

Comment,
Constitutional Protection of Commercial Speech.
82 Colum. L. Rev. 751 (1982)

Comment,
Free Speech, the Private Employee, and State
Constitutions.
91 Yale L.J. 522 (1982)

Comment,
Constitutional Limitations on Body Searches in
Prisons.
82 Colum L. Rev. 1033 (1982)

Comment,
Mistrials Arising From Prosecutorial Error: Double
Jeopardy Protection.
34 Stan. L.Rev. 1061 (1982)

Comment,
Prosecutorial Vindictiveness in the Criminal
Appellate Process: Due process Protection After
United States v. Goodwin.
81 Mich. L. Rev. 194 (1982)

Comment,
The Michigan Malpractice Act's Requirement of a
Physician on the Panel Violates the Due Process
Right to a Fair and Impartial Tribunal.
28 Wayne L. Rev. 1843 (1982)

Comment,
Stone v. Powell and the Effective Assistance of
Counsel.
80 Mich. L. Rev. 1326 (1982)

Article IV
Legislative Branch

VanDusen,
Government Law: State and Local.
30 Wayne L. Rev. 641 (1984)

Article VI
Judicial Branch

Currie,
The Constitution in the Supreme Court: Limitations
on State Power 1865-1873.
51 U. Chi. L. Rev. 329 (1984)

Sinda,
Rules of Evidence: An Exercise of Constitutional
Power by the Michigan Supreme Court.
1980 Det. C.L. Rev. 1063 (1980)

Article VIII
Education

Faxon,
The Need for Constitutional Reform of Michigan's
Higher Educational System.
1983 Det. C.L. Rev. 1209 (1983)

Comment,
The Unconstitutionality of State Statutes
Authorizing Moments of Silence in the Public
Schools.
96 Harv. L. Rev. 1874 (1983)

Article IX
Finance and Taxation

Wethorn,
Taxation: State and Local.
30 Wayne L. Rev. 789 (1984)

MINNESOTA

Chapter Twenty-three
MINNESOTA CONSTITUTION - 1857

Article I
Bill of Rights

Gershel,
Evaluating a Proposed Civil Rights Approach to Pornography: Legal Analysis as if Women Mattered.
11 Wm. Mitchell L. Rev. 41 (1985)

Tigue,
Civil Rights and Censorship--Incompatible Bedfellows.
11 Wm. Mitchell L. Rev. 81 (1985)

Auerbach,
Anatomy of an Unusual Economic Substantive Due Process Case: Workers' Compensation Insurers Rating Association v. State.
68 Minn. L. Rev. 545 (1984)

Fleming,
Minnesota Bill of Rights: "Wrapt in the Old Miasmal Mist."
1984 Hamline L. Rev. 51 (1984)

Fleming,
Minnesota Bill of Rights: Ascending from the Damp Savannas?
54 Hennepin Law. 16 (1984)

Goldberg,
Good Faith Attack on 4th Amendment.
41 Bench & B. 17 (1984)

Mickelsen,
Use and Interpretation of Article I, Section 8 of the Minnesota Constitution 1861-1984.
10 Wm. Mitchell L. Rev. 667 (1984)

McKnight,
Minnesota Rational Relation Test: The Lochner
Monster in the 10,000 Lakes.
10 Wm. Mitchell L. Rev. 709 (1984)

Neville,
Good Faith Exception to the Exclusionary Rule.
10 Minn. Trial Law. 21 (1984)

Marshall,
Solving the Free Exercise Dilemma: Free Exercise
as Expression.
67 Minn. L. Rev. 545 (1983)

Dix,
Means of Executing Searches and Seizures as Fourth
Amendment Issues.
67 Minn. L. Rev. 89 (1982)

Sheran and Isaacman,
Do We Want a Responsible Press?:   A Call for the
Creation of Self-Regulatory Mechanisms.
8 Wm. Mitchell L. Rev. 1 (1982)

Comment,
Discriminatory Property Tax Assessment.
65 Minn. L. Rev. 1089 (1981)

Comment,
Limited Weapons Search.
65 Minn. L. Rev. 1073 (1981)

Comment,
Search of an Attorney's Office.
7 Wm. Mitchell L. Rev. 253 (1981)

Comment,
Warrantless Search by Probation Officer.
65 Minn. L. Rev. 1076 (1981)

Bice,
Rationality Analysis in Constitutional Law.
65 Minn. L. Rev. 1 (1980)

Nemerson,
Coercive Sentencing.
64 Minn. L. Rev. 669 (1980)

Comment,
<u>Criminal   Procedure   -   Warranted   Search   of
Attorney's Office Violates State Constitution</u>.
14 Suffolk U.L. Rev. 186 (1980)

Comment,
<u>Constitutional Propriety of State Judges' Inquiries
Into The Numerical Division of Deadlocked Juries</u>.
64 Minn. L. Rev. 813 (1980)

Comment,
<u>Criminal   Procedure   -   Warranted   Search   of
Attorney's Office Violates State Constitution</u>.
14 Suffolk U.L. Rev. 1185 (1980)

Article VI
Judiciary

Peters,
<u>Symposium on an Intermediate Appellate Court in
Minnesota</u>.
7 Wm. Mitchell L. Rev. 41 (1981)

Stuart,
<u>Legitimacy of Referee Functions</u>.
6 Wm. Mitchell L. Rev. 65 (1980)

Article X
Taxation

Lockhart,
<u>Revolution in State Taxation of Commerce</u>.
65 Minn. L. Rev. 1025 (1981)

Comment,
<u>Real Estate Tax Exemption for Federally Subsidized
Low-Income Housing Corporations</u>.
64 Minn. L. Rev. 1094 (1980)

MISSISSIPPI

Chapter Twenty-four

MISSISSIPPI CONSTITUTION - 1890

Article I
Distribution of Powers

Holwadel,
1983 Mississippi Supreme Court Review:
Administrative Law.
54 Miss. L.J. 46 (1984)

Article III
Bill of Rights

Comment,
1984 Mississippi Supreme Court Review: Wills and
Estates.
55 Miss. L.J. 120 (1985)

Collins,
Reliance on State Constitutions: Some Random
Thoughts.
54 Miss. L.J. 371 (1984)

Forester,
1982 Mississippi Supreme Court Review:
Miscellaneous.
53 Miss. L.J. 179 (1983)

Neyland,
1981 Mississippi Supreme Court Review: Civil
Procedure.
52 Miss. L.J. 399 (1982)

Sledge,
Evidence of Business Factors Probative of Future
Earnings Is Properly Admissible in Condemnation
Proceedings Concerning Certificates of Public
Convenience and Necessity.
52 Miss. L.J. 927 (1982)

Article IV
Legislative Department

Comment,
Conflict of Interest - Public Officials - A Legislator
Guilty of Misdemeanor if He Has Direct Interest in
Contract Authorized by Legislature.
52 Miss. L.J. 659 (1982)

Article VI
Judiciary

Sweat,
1983 Mississippi Supreme Court Review: Civil
Procedure.
54 Miss. L.J. 84 (1984)

Ayers,
1982 Mississippi Supreme Court Review: Criminal
Law and Procedure: No Right to Hold Public Office
After Conviction.
53 Miss. L.J. 155 (1983)

Siler,
1982 Mississippi Supreme Court Review:
Administrative Law: Workmen's Compensation.
53 Miss. L.J. 113 (1983)

Doyel,
Symposium on Mississippi Rules of Civil Procedure:
Pretrial Motions Under the Mississippi Rules of
Civil Procedure--Rules 12 and 56.
52 Miss. L.J. 21 (1982)

Neyland,
1981 Mississippi Supreme Court Review: Civil
Procedure.
52 Miss. L.J. 399 (1982)

Robertson,
Joinder of Claims and Parties--Rules 13, 14, 17 and
18.
52 Miss. L.J. 37 (1982)

MISSOURI

Chapter Twenty-five
MISSOURI CONSTITUTION - 1945

Article I
Bill of Rights

Comment,
Attorney-Client   Communications   of   Criminal
Defendants.
62 Wash. U.L.Q. 739 (1985)

Comment,
Withholding   Lifesaving   Treatment   from   Defective
Newborns: An Equal Protection Analysis.
29 St. Louis U.L.J. 853 (1985)

Milne,
Civil   Jury   Trial--What   do   "Fair"   and   "Impartial"
Mean?
40 J. Mo. B. 543 (1984)

Scurlock,
Arrest,   Searches   and   Seizures,   Privilege   Against
Self-Incrimination.
51 UMKC L. Rev. 401 (1983)

Thomas,
Limits Imposed on Local Governments.
52 UMKC L. Rev. 22 (1983)

Van Patten,
In the End is the Beginning: An inquiry into the
Meaning of the Religion Clauses.
27 St. Louis U.L.J. 1 (1983)

Weissman,
Determinate   Sentencing   and   Psychiatric   Evidence:
Due process Examination.
27 St. Louis U.L.J. 347 (1983)

Comment,
Public Employment Agreements: Enforceability
Issue.
27 St. Louis U.L.J. 981 (1983)

Spiegel,
Inevitable Discovery: An Exception to the
Exclusionary Rule.
38 J. Mo. B. 495 (1982)

Vestal,
Preclusion of Duplicative Prosecutions.
47 Mo. L. Rev. 1 (1982)

Comment,
Judicial Schizophrenia: An Involuntarily Confined
Mental Patient's Right to Refuse Antipsychotic
Drugs.
51 UMKC L. Rev. 76 (1982)

Comment,
Voluntarily Unlocking the Schoolhouse Door: Use
of Class Action Consent Decrees in School
Desegregation.
60 Wash. U.L.Q. 1305 (1982)

Comment,
Fire at Will: An Analysis of the Missouri at Will
Employment Doctrine.
25 St. Louis U.L.J. 845 (1982)

Comment,
Public School Library: Who Will Control?
50 UMKC L. Rev. 567 (1982)

Circo,
Involuntary Psychiatric Treatment and Other
Coercive Behavioral Interventions as Criminal
Sanctions.
59 Wash. U.L.Q. 81 (1981)

Jones, Hardy and Potter,
Deterrence, Retribution, Denunciation and the Death
Penalty.
49 UMKC L. Rev. 158 (1981)

Sirico,
Constitutional   Dimensions   of   CHurch   Property
Disputes.
59 Wash. U.L.Q. 1 (1981)

Comment,
Constitutional   Validity   of   Regulations   Controlling
Noncommercial   Door-to-Door   Canvassing   and
Solicitation.
46 Mo. L. Rev. 121 (1981)

Chase,
Litigating a Nativity Scene Case.
24 St. Louis U.L.J. 237 (1980)

Finch,
Problems and Progress in Press-Bar Conflicts.
36 J. Mo. B. 362 (1980)

Gaffney,
Political Divisiveness Along Religious Lines.
24 St. Louis U.L.J. 205 (1980)

Gard,
Fighting Words as Free Speech.
58 Wash. U.L.Q. 531 (1980)

Loewenthal,
Evaluating   the   Exclusionary   Rule   in   Search   and
Seizure.
49 UMKC L. Rev. 24 (1980)

Pevar,
Public School Christmas Assemblies.
24 St. Louis U.L.J. 273 (1980)

Voelpel,
Material Witness and Material Injustice.
58 Wash. U.L.Q. 1 (1980)

Comment,
Damages Actions for Denial of Equal Educational
Opportunities.
45 Mo. L. Rev. 281 (1980)

Comment,
1978 Pregnancy Discrimination Act: A Problem of
Interpretation.
58 Wash. U.L.Q. 607 (1980)

Comment,
Right of Privacy Challenges to Prostitution Statutes.
58 Wash. U.L.Q. 439 (1980)

Comment,
Courtroom   Closure and the Rights of the Free
Press.
58 Wash. U.L.Q. 945 (1980)

Comment,
The Current Status of the Right of Adult Adoptees
to Know the Identity of Their Natural Parents.
58 Wash. U.L.Q. 677 (1980)

Comment,
Warrantless Murder Scene Searches.
58 Wash. U.L.Q. 367 (1980)

Article II
Distribution of Powers

Comment,
Administrative   Hearing   Commission   and   the
Separation of Powers.
49 Mo. L. Rev. 854 (1984)

Comment,
Comparing   Products   Liability   and   Medical
Malpractice.
24 St. Louis U.L.J. 554 (1980)

Article III
Legislative Department

Comment,
Initiative and Referendum in Missouri.
48 Mo. L. Rev. 991 (1983)

Crosby,
At-large Congressional Elections.
38 J. Mo. B. 266 (1982)

Article V
Judicial Department

Cohen,
Continuing the Court Reform: Eliminating the Trial
De Novo from the Associate Circuit Judge.
39 J. Mo. B. 200 (1983)

Hornstein and Nagle,
State Court Power to Enjoin Federal Judicial
Proceedings: Donovan v. City of Dallas Revisited.
60 Wash. U.L.Q. 1 (1982)

Murphy,
Supreme Court Review of Abstract State Court
Decisions on Federal law: A Justiciability Analysis.
25 St. Louis U.L.J. 473 (1981)

Comment,
Comparing Products Liability and Medical
Malpractice.
24 St. Louis U.L.J. 554 (1980)

Comment,
Constitutional Law: Statutorily Required Mediation
as a Precondition to Lawsuit Denies Access to the
Courts.
45 Mo. L. Rev. 316 (1980)

Article VI
Local Government

Schroeder,
Judicial Notice in Missouri.
48 Mo. L. Rev. 893 (1983)

Thomas,
Local Government Taxation.
49 UMKC L. Rev. 491 (1981)

Article IX
Education

Benson,
Liability of Missouri Suburban School Districts for
Unconstitutional Segregation of Neighboring Urban
School Districts.
53 UMKC L. Rev. 349 (1985)

Comment,
Damages Actions for Denial of Equal Educational
Opportunities.
45 Mo. L. Rev. 281 (1980)

Article X
Taxation

Hoffhaus,
Tax Relief for In Transit Warehouses.
39 J. Mo. B. 21 (1983)

Robertson and Kincheloe,
Missouri's Tax Limitation Amendment.
52 UMKC L. Rev. 1 (1983)

Thomas,
Recent   Developments   in   Missouri: Local
Government Taxation.
49 UMKC L. Rev. 491 (1981)

Article XII
Amending the Constitution

Comment,
Initiative and Referendum in Missouri.
48 Mo. L. Rev. 991 (1983)

MONTANA

Chapter Twenty-six
MONTANA CONSTITUTION - 1972

Article I
Compact With the United States

Elison and NettikSimmons,
Federalism and State Constitutions: The New
Doctrine of Independent and Adequate State
Grounds.
45 Mont. L. Rev. 177 (1984)

Lamb,
Adjudication of Indian Water Rights:
Implementation of the 1979 Amendments to the
Water Use Act.
41 Mont. L. Rev. 39 (1980)

Article II
Declaration of Rights

Elison and Simmons,
Right of Privacy. State v. Long 700 P.2d 153
(Mont. 1985).
48 Mont. L. Rev. 1 (1987)

Carey,
Fair Trial and Free Press: The Courtroom Door
Swings Open.
45 Mont. L. Rev. 323 (1984)

Cromwell,
Federalism and Due Process: Some Ruminations.
42 Cont. L. Rev. 183 (1981)

Huff,
Protecting Due Process and Civic Friendship in the
Administrative State.
42 Mont. L. Rev. 1 (1981)

Reep,
Intrusion, Exclusion, and Confusion.
41 Mont. L. Rev. 281 (1980)

Tobias and McLean,
The Effect of the Environmental Policy Acts on
Pre-Existing Agency Authority.
41 Mont. L. Rev. 177 (1980)

Article VII
The Judiciary

Huff,
The Temptations of Creon: Philosophical
Reflections on the Ethics of the Lawyer's
Professional Role.
46 Mont. L. Rev. 47 (1985)

Alexander,
Making Small Claims Courts Work in Montana:
Recommendations for Legislative and Judicial Action.
45 Mont. L. Rev. 245 (1984)

Alexander,
Small Claims Courts in Montana: A Statistical
Study.
44 Mont. L. Rev. 227 (1983)

Article IX
Environment and Natural Resources

Hightower,
A New Rule of Law for the Abandonment of Water
Rights.
45 Mont. L. Rev. 167 (1984)

Ladd,
Federal and Interstate Conflicts in Montana Water
Law: Support for a State Water Plan.
42 Mont. L. Rev. 267 (1981)

Meissner,
A Constitutional Challenge to the Surface Mining
Control and Reclamation Act.
2 Pub. Land L.Rev. 138 (1981)

Shanahan,
Hardrock Mining on the Public Lands.
2 Pub. Land L. Rev. 57 (1981)

Lamb,
Adjudication of Indian Water Rights:
Implementation of the 1979 Amendments to the
Water Use Act.
41 Mont. L. Rev. 73 (1980)

Morrison,
Comments on Indian Water Rights.
41 Mont. L. Rev. 39 (1980)

Article X
Education and Public Lands

Woodgerd & McCarthy,
State School Trust Lands and Oil and Gas Royalty
Rates.
3 Pub. Land L. Rev. 119 (1982)

NEBRASKA

Chapter Twenty-seven
NEBRASKA CONSTITUTION - 1875

Article I
Bill of Rights

Comment,
Blinding Fundamental Rights With "Bright-Line"
Rules.
64 Neb. L. Rev. 480 (1985)

Kirst,
Nebraska's Modern Service of Process Statute.
63 Neb. L. Rev. 1 (1984)

Comment,
Closing the Gates: A Nebraska Constitutional
Standard For Search and Seizure.
63 Neb. L. Rev. 473 (1984)

Comment,
To Submit or Not to Submit--Where is My
Attorney?: The Right to Counsel Before Submission
to Chemical Testing in a DWI Proceeding.
63 Neb. L. Rev. 373 (1984)

Comment,
Pretrial Hypnosis and Its Effects on Witness
Competency in Criminal Trials.
62 Neb. L. Rev. 336 (1983)

Potuto,
Prison Disciplinary Procedures and Judicial Review
Under the Nebraska Administrative Procedure Act.
61 Neb. L. Rev. 1 (1982)

Simon,
Reporter Privilege: Can Nebraska Pass a Chield
Law to Bind the Whole World?
61 Neb. L. Rev. 446 (1982)

Comment,
Residual Hearsay Exceptions.
61 Neb. L. Rev. 187 (1982)

Comment,
Sufficiency of Circumstantial Evidence in Nebraska
Civil Cases: What Is the Test?
60 Neb. L. Rev. 636 (1981)

Article III
Legislative Power

Comment,
Nebraska Unicameral Rule 3, Section 15: To Whom
Must the Door Be Open?
64 Neb. L. Rev. 282 (1985)

Comment,
Nebraska's Legislative Responses to the Energy
Crisis: Solar Energy, Gasohol, and the Conservation
Ethic.
60 Neb. L. Rev. 327 (1981)

Article V
Judicial

Comment,
Medical Malpractice Statute of Repose: An
Unconstitutional Denial of Access to the Courts.
63 Neb. L. Rev. 150 (1984)

Article VII
Education

Davidson,
State Appropriations to Private Schools: Can the
Legislature Contract out of the Constitution?
64 Neb. L. Rev. 444 (1985)

Comment,
School Health Services for Handicapped Children:
The Door Opens No Further.
64 Neb. L. Rev. 509 (1985)

Comment,
Constitutionality of State Tax Deductions for
Private School Tuition: A New Door In The Wall of
Separation.
63 Neb. L. Rev. 572 (1984)

Article VIII
Revenue

Comment,
Unitary Taxation: An Analysis of State Taxation of
Multijurisdictional Corporations in Nebraska.
64 Neb. L. Rev. 135 (1985)

Comment,
Separate Property Tax Classification for Agricultural
Land: Cure or Disease?
64 Neb. L. Rev. 313 (1985)

Comment,
State Taxation of Multinational Corporations and
the Apportionment of Worldwide Income.
63 Neb. L. Rev. 631 (1984)

Comment,
Constitutionality of State Tax Deductions for
Private School Tuition: A New Door In The Wall of
Separation.
63 Neb. L. Rev. 572 (1984)

Article XII
Miscellaneous Corporations

Comment,
Unitary Taxation: An Analysis of State Taxation of
Multijurisdictional Corporations in Nebraska.
64 Neb. L. Rev. 135 (1985)

Comment,
State Taxation of Multinational Corporations and
the Apportionment of Worldwide Income.
63 Neb. L. Rev. 631 (1984)

Comment,
At the Crossroads of Corporate Takeover
Legislation.
63 Neb. L. Rev. 345 (1984)

Article XVI
Amendments

Comment,
An Equal Protection Analysis of the Classifications
in Initiative 300: The Family Farm Amendment to
the Constitution of the State of Nebraska.
62 Neb. L. Rev. 770 (1983)

NEVADA

Chapter Twenty-eight

NEVADA CONSTITUTION - 1864

Article I
Declaration of Rights

Lucas,
Pre-Trial Habeas Corpus in Nevada: The Mistake of
Res Judicata.
48 Inter Alia 1(1) (1982-1983)

Article III
Distribution of Powers

Lucas,
Pre-Trial Habeas Corpus in Nevada: The Mistake of
Res Judicata.
48 Inter Alia 1(1) (1982-1983)

Wooster,
Nevada Constitutional Law: The Problem of Special
and Local Legislation.
43 Inter Alia 20(2) (1978)

Article IV
Legislative Department

Titus,
The Nevada "Sagebrush Rebellion" Act: A Question
of Constitutionality.
23 Ariz. L. Rev. 264 (1981)

Wooster,
Nevada Constitutional Law: The Problem of Special
and Local Legislation.
43 Inter Alia 20(2) (1978)

Article VI
Judicial Department

Lucas,
Pre-Trial Habeas Corpus in Nevada: The Mistake of
Res Judicata.
48 Inter Alia 1(1) (1982-1983)

Article VIII
Corporations

Belford,
The Decline and Fall of Stockholders' Limited
Liability in Nevada.
40 Inter Alia 3(3) (1975)

NEW HAMPSHIRE

Chapter Twenty-nine
NEW HAMPSHIRE CONSTITUTION - 1784

Part First
Bill of Rights

Comment,
Stanley D. v. Deborah D.: An Analysis of Child
Custody.
27 N.H. B.J. 85 (1986)

Hutchins,
The "Intentional Act" Exclusion in New Hampshire
After MacKinnon v. Hanover Insurance Co.
26 N.H. B.J. 221 (1985)

Wiebusch,
New Hampshire Civil Practice and Procedures.
25 N.H. B.J. 277 (1984)

Clyons,
Bright Lines on the Highway: The Demand for
Specificity in Relation to the Warrant Requirement.
24 N.H. B.J. 145 (1983)

Reardon,
Some Current Thoughts on First Amendment
Problems.
23 N.H. B.J. 30 (1982)

Kfoury,
Termination of Parental Rights in New Hampshire.
23 N.H. B.J. 10 (1981)

Rair,
Downing v. Monitor Publishing Co.: The Use of a
Presumption to Compel Disclosure of Sources in
Libel Cases.
22 N.H. B.J. 82 (1981)

Part Second
Form of Government

Jenkins,
Trees and the Law in New Hampshire.
25 N.H. B.J. 9 (1983)

Stocklin-Enright,
Constitutionalism and the Rule of Law: New
Hampshire's Home Schooling Quandry.
8 Vermont L. Rev. 265 (1983)

Marsan,
Interest-Free   Demand   Loans: Income   Tax
Implications Between Corporations and Shareholders
or Employees.
22 N.H. B.J. 94 (1981)

DeGrandpre,
Lex Loci: Recent New Hampshire Supreme Court
Decisions.
22 N.H. B.J. 8 (1980)

NEW JERSEY

Chapter Thirty
NEW JERSEY CONSTITUTION - 1947

Article I
Rights and Privileges

Devine and Feldman,
Death penalty in New Jersey--Constitutionality.
15 Rutgers L.J. 261 (1984)

Drakeman,
Voluntary Religious Activities in the Public Schools.
14 Seton Hall L. Rev. 252 (1984)

Greenberg,
New Jersey's "Fairness and Rightness" Doctrine.
15 Rutgers L. Rev. 927 (1984)

Rodriguez,
Proportionality Review in New Jersey: An
Indispensable Safeguard in the Capital Sentencing
Process.
15 Rutgers L.J. 399 (1984)

Vesper,
Understanding Juries.
113 N.J. L.J. 713 (1984)

Comment,
Free Press--A State Constitutional Right of Access
to Pretrial Hearings.
14 Seton Hall L. Rev. 788 (1984)

Comment,
Establishment   Clause--Tax   Benefits   to   Parents
Whose Children Attend Sectarian Schools.
14 Seton Hall L. Rev. 683 (1984)

Comment,
Search and Seizure - School Officials May Conduct
Student Searches Upon Satisfaction of
Reasonableness Test.
14 Seton Hall L. Rev. 738 (1984)

Comment,
Tasting the Fruit of the Poisonous Tree.
36 Rutgers L. Rev. 346 (1983-84)

Comment,
Triumph of the Press: New Jersey Departs From
Federal Trends in Libel Law.
36 Rutgers L. Rev. 91 (1983-1984)

Humbach,
Just-Compensation Cases: Takings, Regulation and
Public Use.
34 Rutgers L.J. 243 (1982)

Levine,
Toward Competent Counsel.
13 Rutgers L.J. 227 (1982)

Comment,
Increase in Sentence after Partially Served Custodial
Term Violative of Double Jeopardy Clause.
12 Seton Hall L. Rev. 291 (1982)

Comment,
Fourth Amendment Warrant Standards For
Immigration Search of Business Premises for
Undocumented Aliens.
13 Rutgers L.J. 607 (1982)

Comment,
First Amendment Right of Access to Government-
Held Information.
34 Rutgers L.J. 292 (1982)

Comment,
Sixth Amendment LImitations on the Newsperson's
Privilege.
13 Rutgers L.J. 361 (1982)

Arenella,
Reforming the State Grand Jury System: A Model
Grand Jury Act.
13 Rutgers L.J. 1 (1981)

Bloustein,
Freedom   of   Expression--Origin,   Validity,   and
Interrelationships of the Political Values.
33 Rutgers L. Rev. 372 (1981)

Bloustein,
Why   is   Freedom   of   Speech   a   Problem   in
Contemporary America?
13 Rutgers L.J. 59 (1981)

Blumrosen,
Affirmative Action in Employment After Weber.
34 Rutgers L.J. 1 (1981)

Gardner,
Right to be Punished.
33 Rutgers L. Rev. 838 (1981)

Comment,
Court of Equity Has Inherent Power to Exercise
Mentally Retarded Individual's Right to Sterilization.
12 Seton Hall L. Rev. 96 (1981)

Comment,
Functional Literacy Testing and Denial of High
School Diplomas.
33 Rutgers L. Rev. 564 (1981)

Comment,
The Hyde Amendment: An Infringement Upon The
Free Exercise Clause.
33 Rutgers L. Rev. 1054 (1981)

Comment,
Judicial Dilemma: Extension or Invalidation of
Sexually Discriminatory Classifications.
34 Rutgers L.J. 128 (1981)

Comment,
Burden of Persuasion Shifts In Remedial Claim After
Funding of Sexual Harassment in Work Environment.
11 Seton Hall L. Rev. 825 (1981)

Comment,
Fact and Opinion After Gertz v. Robert Welch, Inc.
34 Rutgers L.J. 81 (1981)

Comment,
Right of Access to Private Property Independent of
Federal Constitution.
12 Seton Hall L. Rev. 76 (1981)

Comment,
NLRB v. ILA: Technological Change and the Work
preservation Doctrine.
33 Rutgers L. Rev. 1108 (1981)

Comment,
Secondary Picketing – The Pruning of the Tree
Fruits Exception.
11 Seton Hall L. Rev. 519 (1981)

Comment,
Stop and Identify Statutes.
12 Rutgers L.J. 585 (1981)

Comment,
Rights of Student Religious Groups Under The First
Amendment to Hold Meetings on Public University
Campus.
33 Rutgers L. Rev. 1008 (1981)

Parker,
Sex Discrimination and the New Jersey Constitution
after Peper v. Princeton.
6 Women's Rights L.Rep. 133 (1980)

Stone,
Criminal Justice System and the News Media.
7 Crim. Just. Q. 178 (1980)

Tener,
1974 Amendments to New Jersey Employer-Employee
Relations Act.
11 Rut.-Cam. L.J. 177 (1980)

Comment,
Developing an Equal Protection Standard for Gender
Discrimination Cases.
11 Rut.-Cam. L.J. 293 (1980)

Comment,
Personal Letters: A Dilemma For Copyright and
Privacy Law.
33 Rutgers L. Rev. 134 (1980)

Comment,
Sincere Religious Belief, Though Not a Tenet of
One's Church or Sect, Still Protected by First
Amendment.
11 Seton Hall L. Rev. 220 (1980)

Comment,
Establishment Clause, Teaching of Science of
Creative Intelligence/Transcendental Meditation in
Public Schools Violates Establishment Clause of
First Amendment.
10 Seton Hall L. Rev. 614 (1980)

Comment,
Defamation: Conflict in the Definition of "Public
Figure."
10 Seton Hall L. Rev. 822 (1980)

Comment,
Complexity of Case May Justify Denial of Jury Trial.
12 Rutgers L.J. 377 (1980)

Comment,
Implied Consent laws: Some Unsettled
Constitutional Questions.
12 Rutgers L.J. 99 (1980)

Comment,
Admission of Non Testifying Codefendant's
Statement Not Violative of Nondeclarant's
Confrontation Rights by Admission of Nontestifying
Codefendants.
10 Seton Hall L. Rev. 630 (1980)

Article III
Distribution of the Powers of Government

Comment,
Public Question No. Seven; a Threat to the
Constitution's Balance of Power.
116 N.J. L.J. 4 (1985)

Byrne,
Role of the judiciary in the Modern Institutional
State.
11 Seton Hall L. Rev. 643 (1981)

Article IV
Legislative

Donnelly,
Junkets--Regulation of Casino Marketing Under the
Casino Control Act.
6 Seton Hall Legis.J. 71 (1982)

Hawking,
Casino Gambling as an Economic Recovery Program.
6 Seton Hall Legis.J. 1 (1982)

Lampen,
Role of legalized Gaming as a Stimulus for Tourism
and Urban Redevelopment.
6 Seton Hall Legis.J. 55 (1982)

Santaniello,
Casino Gambling: Elements of Effective Control.
6 Seton Hall Legis.J. 23 (1982)

Comment,
Voters' Right to Approve State Debt.
33 Rutgers L. Rev. 198 (1980)

Article VI
Judicial

King,
Constitutionality of No Fault Jurisprudence.
4 Utah L. Rev. 797 (1982)

Comment,
Entire Controversy Doctrine.
12 Seton Hall L. Rev. 260 (1982)

Byrne,
Role of the Judiciary in the Modern Institutional
State.
11 Seton Hall L. Rev. 653 (1981)

Article VIII
Taxation and Finance

Weinberg,
Coastal Area Legislation.
6 Seton Hall Legis.J. 317 (1983)

Guard and LaMaita,
Financing Public Educational Facilities After the
Freehold Decision.
12 Seton Hall L. Rev. 195 (1982)

Comment,
Future of Farmland and Preservation.
12 Rutgers L.J. 713 (1981)

Comment,
Education of Illegal Alien Children.
11 Seton Hall L. Rev. 499 (1981)

Comment,
Voters' Right to Approve State Debt.
33 Rutgers L. Rev. 198 (1980)

Article XI
Schedule

King,
Constitutionality of No Fault Jurisprudence.
4 Utah L. Rev. 797 (1982)

NEW MEXICO

Chapter Thirty-one
NEW MEXICO CONSTITUTION - 1911

Article II
Bill of Rights

Comment,
Development of Modern Libel law: A Philosophic
Analysis.
16 N.M.L. Rev. 183 (1986)

Comment,
Criminal   Procedure   -   Search   and   Seizure   -
Expectations of Privacy in the Open Fields and an
Evolving Fourth Amendment Standard of Legitimacy:
Oliver v. United States.
16 N.M.L. Rev. 129 (1986)

Comment,
Annual Survey of New Mexico Property Law.
16 N.M.L. Rev. 59 (1986)

Comment,
Annual Survey of New Mexico Criminal Law.
16 N.M.L. Rev. 9 (1986)

Comment,
Annual Survey of New Mexico Criminal Procedure.
16 N.M.L. Rev. 25 (1986)

Comment,
Development of Modern Libel Law: A Philosophic
Analysis.
16 N.M.L. Rev. 183 (1986)

Comment,
Annual Survey of New Mexico Employment Law.
16 N.M.L. Rev. 39 (1986)

Browde,
Separation of Powers and the Judicial Rule-Making
Power in New Mexico: The Need for Prudential
Restraints.
15 N.M.L. Rev. 407 (1985)

Higdon,
Defamation in New Mexico.
14 N.M.L. Rev. 321 (1984)

Holt,
Survey of New Mexico Law, 1982-83: Criminal
Procedure.
14 N.M.L. Rev. 109 (1984)

Comment,
Compulsory School Attendance--Who Directs the
Education of a Child? State v. Edgington.
14 N.M.L. Rev. 453 (1984)

Comment,
Procedural and Substantive Rights to the Media
Govern Requests to Restrict News Coverage of
Criminal Cases: State ex rel. New Mexico Press
Ass'n v. Kaufman.
14 N.M.L. Rev. 401 (1984)

Comment,
Search and Seizure: The Automobile Exception to
the Fourth Amendment Warrant Requirement--A
Further Exception to the Fourth: State v. Capps.
14 N.M.L. Rev. 239 (1984)

Silver,
Constitutionality of the New Mexico Capital
Punishment Statute.
11 N.M.L. Rev. 269 (1981)

Article III
Distribution of Powers

Comment,
Annual Survey of New Mexico Criminal Procedure.
16 N.M.L. Rev. 25 (1986)

Browde,
Separation of Powers and the Judicial Rule-Making
Power in New Mexico: The Need for Prudential
Restraints.
15 N.M.L. Rev. 407 (1985)

Article IV
Legislative Department

Browde,
Separation of Powers and the Judicial Rule-Making
Power in New Mexico: The Need for Prudential
Restraints.
15 N.M.L. Rev. 407 (1985)

Article VI
Judicial Department

Browde,
Separation of Powers and the Judicial Rule-Making
Power in New Mexico: The Need for Prudential
Restraints.
15 N.M.L. Rev. 407 (1985)

Comment,
The Subject Matter Jurisdiction of New Mexico
District Courts Over Civil Cases Involving Indians.
15 N.M.L. Rev. 75 (1985)

Article XI
Corporations Other Than Municipal

Kelly,
Survey of New Mexico Law, 1982-83: Administrative
Law.
14 N.M.L. Rev. 1 (1984)

NEW YORK

Chapter Thirty-two
NEW YORK CONSTITUTION - 1982

Comment,
Compelled production of Corporate Papers After
Fisher and Doe.
54 Fordham L. Rev. 935 (1986)

Bender,
The Takings Clause: Principles or Politics?
34 Buffalo L. Rev. 735 (1985)

Comment,
Grandparents Versus the State: A Constitutional
Right to Custody.
13 Hofstra L. Rev. 375 (1985)

Comment,
The Right of Self-Representation in the Capital
Case.
85 Colum. L. Rev. 130 (1985)

Comment,
Unauthorized Conduct of State Officials Under the
Fourteenth Amendment: Hudson v. Palmer and the
Resurrection of Dead Doctrine.
85 Colum. L. Rev. 837 (1985)

Berger,
The Psychiatric Expert as Due Process Decision
Maker.
33 Buffalo L. Rev. 681 (1984)

Wackerman,
The Due Process Rights of Foster Parents.
50 Brooklyn L. Rev. 483 (1984)

Comment,
Washington   v.   Strickland: Defining   Effective
Assistance of Counsel at Capital Sentencing.
83 Colum. L. Rev. 1544 (1983)

Hill,
Testimonial Privilege and Fair Trial.
80 Colum. L. Rev. 1173 (1980)

Article I
Bill of Rights

Bellacosa,
A New York State Constitution Touch of Class.
195 N.Y. L.J. 26 (1986)

Lushing,
The Exclusionary Rule; A Disputation.
7 Cardozo L. Rev. 713 (1986)

Ragosta,
Free Speech Access to Shopping Malls Under State
Constitutions: Analysis and Rejection.
37 Syracuse L. Rev. 1 (1986)

Comment,
Public   Forum   Analysis   After   Perry   Educational
Association v.   Perry   Local   Educators'   Association-
A   Conceptual   Approach   to   Claims   of   First
Amendment Access to Publicly Owned Property.
54 Fordham L. Rev. 545 (1986)

Comment,
Dragnet Drug Testing in Public Schools and the
Fourth Amendment.
86 Colum. L. Rev. 852 (1986)

Comment,
Fair Comment and Music Criticism: New York Law
Under the Constitutional Defenses to Libel.
37 Syracuse L. Rev. 79 (1986)

Comment,
Vertical   and   Horizontal   Aspects   of   Takings
Jurisprudence: Is Airspace Property?
7 Cardozo L. Rev. 489 (1986)

Comment,
Police Created Exigencies: Implications for the
Fourth Amendment.
37 Syracuse L. Rev. 147 (1986)

Comment,
Fifth Amendment Privilege and Compelled production
of Corporate Papers After Fisher and Doe.
54 Fordham L. Rev. 935 (1986)

Balsam,
The Media's Right to Refuse Advertising.
3 N.Y.U. Ann. Surv. Am. L. 699 (1985)

Bender,
The Takings Clause: Principles or Politics?
34 Buffalo L. Rev. 735 (1985)

Bjorkman,
From Lehman to Smith haven Mall: Evolving Federal
and State Restrictions on Political Advertising.
3 N.Y.U. Ann. Surv. Am. L. 713 (1985)

Calloway,
Equal Employment and Third Party Privacy
Interests: And Analytical Framework for
Reconciling Competing Rights.
54 Fordham L. Rev. 327 (1985)

Cannon,
First Amendment--The Religion Clauses.
2 N.Y.U. Ann. Surv. Am. L. 265 (1985)

Curtis,
Advertising Regulated Products.
3 N.Y.U. Ann. Surv. Am. L. 621 (1985)

Doberman,
Advertising for Abortion Services and
Contraceptives.
3 N.Y.U. Ann. Surv. Am. L. 655 (1985)

Handler,
First Amendment--Commercial Speech; Free Speech
and the Public Employee.
2 N.Y.U. Ann. Surv. Am. L. 291 (1985)

Neiselman,
The Regulation of Outdoor Advertising: Balancing
Freedom of Speech and Aesthetics.
3 N.Y.U. Ann. Surv. Am. L. 671 (1985)

Comment,
Lynch v. Donnelly: Breaking Down the Barriers to
Religious Displays.
71 Cornell L. Rev. 185 (1985)

Comment,
The Right of Self-Representation in the Capital
Case.
85 Colum. L. Rev. 130 (1985)

Comment,
Unauthorized Conduct of State Officials Under the
Fourteenth Amendment: Hudson v. Palmer and the
Resurrection of Dead Doctrine.
85 Colum. L. Rev. 837 (1985)

Comment,
Private Lives and Public Concerns: The Decade
Since Gertz v. Robert Welch, Inc.
51 Brooklyn L. Rev. 425 (1985)

Comment,
Symposium on Defamation in Fiction.
51 Brooklyn L. Rev. 223 (1985)

Comment,
The Effect of Gaeta v. New York News, Inc. on
New York's Private Libel Plaintiffs.
50 Alb. L. Rev. 157 (1985)

Comment,
The First Amendment and Legislative Bans of Liquor
and Cigarette Advertisements.
85 Colum. L. Rev. 632 (1985)

Comment,
The Supreme Court Creates New Hurdle for Libel
Defendants: Dun & Bradstreet, Inc. v. Greenmoss
Builders, Inc.
60 St. John's L. Rev. 144 (1985)

Comment,
Imprisoning Indigents for Failure to Pay Fine--
Bearden v. Georgia.
30 N.Y.L. Sch. L. Rev. 111 (1985)

Comment,
Abandonment of the Two-Pronged Aguilar-Spinelli
Test: Illinois v. Gates.
70 Cornell L. Rev. 316 (1985)

Comment,
Grandparents Versus the State: A Constitutional
Right to Custody.
13 Hofstra L. Rev. 375 (1985)

Comment,
The Fourth Amendment in the Age of Aerial
Surveillance: Curtains for the Curtilage?
60 N.Y.L. Sch. L. Rev. 725 (1985)

Comment,
The Implications of Leon in the Aftermath of
Gates: The Good Faith Exception in Cases
Involving Reliance on Warrants Issued on the Basis
of hearsay Information.
49 Alb. L. Rev. 1032 (1985)

Comment,
Search and Seizure-Detention of Personal Property
for Investigative Purposes--United States v. Place.
30 N.Y.L. Sch. L. Rev. 139 (1985)

Committee On Education And The Law,
Due Process In Decisions Relating to Tenure in
Higher Education.
39 Rec. 392 (1984)

Berger,
The Psychiatric Expert as Due Process Decision
Maker.
33 Buffalo L. Rev. 681 (1984)

Elder,
Defamation, Public Officialdom and the Rosenblatt v.
Baer Criteria--A Proposal for Revivification Two
Decades After New York Times Co. v. Sullivan.
33 Buffalo L. Rev. 579 (1984)

Kaufman,
Press Privacy and Malice: Reflections on New York
Times v. Sullivan.
5 Cardozo L. Rev. 867 (1984)

Leventhal and Rosenthal,
Standing of a Passenger to Suppress Evidence and
the New York Presumption.
35 Brooklyn B. 145 (1984)

Levine,
The Second Circuit Constricts the Applicability of
the Exclusionary Rule.
50 Brooklyn L. Rev. 601 (1984)

Wackerman,
The Due Process Rights of Foster Parents.
50 Brooklyn L. Rev. 483 (1984)

Comment,
Regional Banking Statutes and the Equal Protection
Clause.
84 Colum. L. Rev. 2025 (1984)

Comment,
Due Process: Application of the Parratt Doctrine to
Random and Unauthorized Deprivations of Life and
Liberty.
52 Fordham L. Rev. 887 (1984)

Comment,
Access to pretrial Documents Under the First
Amendment.
84 Colum. L. Rev. 1813 (1984)

Comment,
The Privacy Plight of Public Employees.
13 Hofstra L. Rev. 189 (1984)

Comment,
Constitutional Law--Fourth Amendment--Plain View
Exception to the Warrant Requirement--Exigent
Circumstances--Washington v. Chrisman.
29 N.Y.L. Sch. L. Rev. 153 (1984)

Comment,
Establishing a Right to Shelter for the Homeless.
50 Brooklyn L. Rev. 939 (1984)

Stewart,
The Road to Mapp v. Ohio and Beyond: The Origins, Development and Future of the Exclusionary Rule in Search-and-Seizure Cases.
83 Colum. L. Rev. 1365 (1983)

Comment,
Washington v. Strickland: Defining Effective Assistance of Counsel at Capital Sentencing.
83 Colum. L. Rev. 1544 (1983)

Comment,
Civil Rights--Employment Discrimination--Sex Based Compensation Discrimination--County of Washington v. Gunther.
28 N.Y.L. Sch. L. Rev. 149 (1983)

Comment,
A Prisoner's Constitutional Right to Attorney Assistance.
83 Colum. L. Rev. 1279 (1983)

King,
Constitutionality of No Fault Jurisprudence.
4 Utah L. Rev. 797 (1982)

Comment,
Warrantless Vehicle Searches and the Fourth Amendment: The Burger Court Attacks the Exclusionary Rule.
68 Cornell L. Rev. 105 (1982)

Alstyne,
The First Amendment and the Free Press: A Comment on Some New Trends and Some Old Theories.
9 Hofstra L. Rev. 1 (1981)

Jackson,
The Primacy of Collective Bargaining for Resolving Disputes Under the Fair Labor Standards Act.
66 Cornell L. Rev. 193 (1981)

Donnino,
Exigent Circumstances for a Warrantless Home Arrest.
45 Alb. L. Rev. 90 (1980)

Hill,
Testimonial Privilege and Fair Trial.
80 Colum. L. Rev. 1173 (1980)

Comment,
Double   Jeopardy: An   Illusory   Remedy   for
Governmental Overreaching at Trial.
29 Buffalo L. Rev. 759 (1980)

Article III
Legislative Power

Givens,
A   Primer   on   the   New   York   State   Legislative
Process: How It Differs From Federal Procedure.
57 N.Y. Sch. B.J. 8 (1985)

Pantaleoni,
New   York's   Real   Property   Tax   Exemption   for
Religious,   Educational,   and   Charitable   Institutions:
A Critical Examination.
44 Alb. L. Rev. 488 (1980)

Sigal,
The   Proposed   Constitutional   Amendments   to   the
Local Finance Article: A Critical Analysis.
8 Fordham Urb. L.J. 29 (1980)

Comment,
Local Finance: A Brief Constitutional History.
8 Fordham Urb. L.J. 135 (1980)

Article VI
Judiciary

Radigan,
Jurisdiction after Piccione.
56 N.Y. Sch. B.J. 12 (1984)

Comment,
Establishing a Right to Shelter for the Homeless.
50 Brooklyn L. Rev. 939 (1984)

Article IX
Local Governments

Cole,
Constitutional Home Rule in New York: "The Ghost
of Home Rule."
59 St. John's L. Rev. 713 (1985)

Comment,
Home Rule and the Sherman Act after Boulder:
Cities Between a Rock and a Hard Place.
49 Brooklyn L. Rev. 259 (1983)

Harper,
The Fordham Symposium on the Local Finance
Project of the Association of the Bar of the City of
New York: An Introductory Essay.
8 Fordham Urb. L.J. 1 (1980)

Sigal,
The Proposed Constitutional Amendments to the
Local Finance Article: A Critical Analysis.
8 Fordham Urb. L.J. 29 (1980)

Comment,
Local Finance: A Brief Constitutional History.
8 Fordham Urb. L.J. 135 (1980)

NORTH CAROLINA

Chapter Thirty-three
NORTH CAROLINA CONSTITUTION- 1970

Article I
Declaration of Rights

Curtis,
Obscenity: The Justices' (Not So) New Robes.
8 Campbell L. Rev. 387 (1986)

Exum,
Dusting Off Our State Constitution.
33 N.C. St. B.Q. 6(3) (1986)

Greenawalt,
The Concept of Religion in State Constitutions.
8 Campbell L. Rev. 437 (1986)

Comment,
Delconte v. State: Some Thoughts on Home
Educations.
64 N.C.L. Rev. 1302 (1986)

Comment,
Wilder v. Amatex Corp.: A First Step Toward
Ameliorating the Effect of Statutes of Repose on
Plaintiffs with Delayed Manifestation Diseases.
64 N.C.L. Rev. 416 (1986)

Ragland,
When is a Confession Coerced and When Is It
Voluntary.
63 N.C.L. Rev. 1214 (1985)

Rhew,
Double Jeopardy and Substantial Rights in North
Carolina Appeals.
63 N.C.L. Rev. 1061 (1985)

Connor,
Survey of 1982 Law on Criminal Procedure.
61 N.C.L. Rev. 1090 (1983)

DiGiovanni,
Survey of 1982 Law on Evidence.
61 N.C.L. Rev. 1126 (1983)

Orth,
Separation of Powers in North Carolina.
62 N.C.L. Rev. 1 (1983)

Parker,
Survey of 1982 Law Relating to Constitutional law.
61 N.C.L. Rev. 1052 (1983)

Geer,
Survey of 1981 Constitutional Law.
60 N.C.L. Rev. 1272 (1982)

Martin,
Freedom of Speech Rights in North Carolina Prior
to Gitlow v. New York.
4 Campbell L. Rev. 243 (1982)

Weissman,
Sentencing Due Process: Evolving Constitutional
Principles.
18 Wake Forest L. Rev. 523 (1982)

Garrett,
Survey of 1987 Tort Law.
59 N.C.L. Rev. 1239 (1981)

Harbison,
Survey of 1980 Constitutional Law.
59 N.C.L. Rev. 1116 (1981)

Comment,
Rape Victim Shield Statute.
3 Campbell L. Rev. 113 (1981)

Markham,
A Powerless Judiciary?   The North Carolina Courts'
Perceptions of Review of Administrative Action.
12 N.C. Cent. L.J. 21 (1980)

Comment,
Sectarian Education and the State.
1980 Duke L.J. 801 (1980)

Comment,
State Regulation of Public Solicitation for Religious
Purposes.
16 Wake Forest L. Rev. 996 (1980)

Comment,
The State and Sectarian Education: Regulation to
Deregulation.
1980 Duke L.J. 801 (1980)

Comment,
State Regulation of Private Religious Schools.
16 Wake Forest L. Rev. 405 (1980)

Comment,
Capital Sentencing Statute.
16 Wake Forest L. Rev. 765 (1980)

Comment,
Directed Verdicts in Favor of the Party with the
Burden of Proof.
16 Wake Forest L. Rev. 607 (1980)

Comment,
Specific Performance of Separation Agreements.
58 N.C.L. Rev. 867 (1980)

Article II
Legislative

Comment,
Sunbathers Versus Property Owners: Public Access
to North Carolina Beaches.
64 N.C.L. Rev. 159 (1985)

Parker,
Survey of 1982 Law Relating to Constitutional Law.
61 N.C.L. Rev. 1052 (1983)

Brown,
Survey of 1979 Administrative Law.
58 N.C.L. Rev. 1185 (1980)

Article III
Executive

Beard,
Survey of 1980 Law on Civil Procedure.
59 N.C.L. Rev. 1067 (1981)

Dickson,
Advisory Rulings by Administrative Agencies: Their
Benefits and Dangers.
2 Campbell L. Rev. 1 (1980)

Laurence,
Removing Local Elected Officials From Office in
North Carolina.
16 Wake Forest L. Rev. 547 (1980)

Article IV
Judiciary

Clark,
The Discipline and Removal of Judges in North
Carolina.
4 Campbell L. Rev. 1 (1981)

Markham,
A Powerless Judiciary?   The North Carolina Courts'
Perceptions of Review of Administrative Action.
12 N.C. Cent. L.J. 21 (1980)

Patrick,
Toward a Codification of the law of Evidence in
North Carolina.
16 Wake Forest L. Rev. 669 (1980)

Stick,
Survey of 1979 Law on Criminal Procedure.
58 N.C.L. Rev. 1404 (1980)

Walker,
The 1980 Amendments to the Federal Rules of Civil
Procedure   and   Proposals   for   North   Carolina
Practice.
16 Wake Forest L. Rev. 915 (1980)

Article V
Finance

Comment,
All the News That's Fit to Tax: First Amendment
Limitations on State and Local Taxation of the
Press.
21 Wake Forest L. Rev. 59 (1985)

Comment,
North Carolina Sales and Use Tax Exemption for
Newspapers, in Light of In Re Village Publishing
Corp.
21 Wake Forest L. Rev. 145 (1985)

Deivey,
Survey of 1980 Tax Law.
59 N.C.L. Rev. 1233 (1981)

Mercer,
Avoiding Another Proposition 13: The Need to
Reform North Carolina Property Tax Law.
59 N.C.L. Rev. 675 (1981)

Comment,
Rejection of the Public Purpose Requirement for
State Tax Exemption.
17 Wake Forest L. Rev. 293 (1981)

Lawrence,
Removing Local Elected Officials From Office in
North Carolina.
16 Wake Forest L. Rev. 547 (1980)

Stipe,
A Decade of Preservation and Preservation Law.
11 N.C. Cent. L.J. 214 (1980)

Article VI
Suffrage and Eligibility to Office

Govert,
Something There Is That Doesn't Love a Wall:
Reflections on the History of North Carolina's
Religious Test for Public Office.
64 N.C.L. Rev. 1071 (1986)

Article VII
Local Government

Erichlow,
Competitive   Annexation   Among   Municipalities:
North Carolina Adopts the Prior Jurisdiction Rule.
63 N.C.L. Rev. 1260 (1985)

Comment,
North Carolina's Unilateral Annexation Statutes.
19 Wake Forest L. Rev. 215 (1983)

Article VIII
Corporations

Geer,
Survey of 1981 Constitutional Law.
60 N.C.L. Rev. 1272 (1982)

Harbinson,
Survey of 1980 Constitutional law.
59 N.C.L. Rev. 1116 (1981)

Comment,
The State and Sectarian Education: Regulation to
Deregulation.
1980 Duke L.J. 801 (1980)

Article IX
Education

Comment,
Delconte v. State: Some Thoughts on Home
Education.
64 N.C.L. Rev. 1302 (1986)

Comment,
Fines, Penalties, and Forfeitures: An Historical and
Comparative Analysis.
65 N.C.L. Rev. 49 (1986)

Comment,
State Regulation of Private Religious Schools.
16 Wake Forest L. Rev. 405 (1980)

Article X
Homesteads and Exemptions

Comment,
The Status of the Presumption of Purchase Money
Resulting Trust for Wives in Light of Mims v. Mims.
61 N.C.L. Rev. 576 (1983)

Reppy,
North Carolina's Tenancy by the Entirety Reform
Legislation of 1982.
5 Campbell L. Rev. 1 (1982)

Weissman,
Sentencing Due Process: Evolving Constitutional
Principles.
18 Wake Forest L. Rev. 523 (1982)

Comment,
The Tax Effects of Equitable Distribution Upon
Divorce.
18 Wake Forest L. Rev. 555 (1982)

Peeples,
North Carolina's New Exemption Act.
17 Wake Forest L. Rev. 865 (1981)

Sharp,
Divorce and the Third Party: Spousal Support,
Private Arrangements and the State.
59 N.C.L. Rev. 819 (1981)

Vukowich,
Debtors' Exemption Rights Under the Bankruptcy
Reform Act.
58 N.C.L. Rev. 769 (1980)

Comment,
Enforcement of Separation Agreements by Specific
Performance.
16 Wake Forest L. Rev. 117 (1980)

Comment,
Tenancy by the Entirety in North Carolina.
59 N.C.L. Rev. 997 (1980)

Article XI
Punishments, Corrections, and Charities

Lindsay,
Prosecutorial Abuse of Peremptory Challenges in
Death Penalty Litigation: Some Constitutional and
Ethical Considerations.
8 Campbell L. Rev. 71 (1985)

Article XII
Military Forces

Comment,
Rejection of the "Public Purpose" Requirement for
State Tax Exemption.
17 Wake Forest L. Rev. 293 (1981)

NORTH DAKOTA

Chapter Thirty-four
NORTH DAKOTA CONSTITUTION- 1889

Article I
Declaration of Rights

Boughey,
An Introduction to North Dakota Constitutional Law:
Content and Methods of Interpretation.
63 N.D.L. Rev. 157 (1987)

Dickson,
The Statute of Limitations in North Dakota's
Products Liability Act: An Exercise in Futility?
59 N.D.L. Rev. 551 (1983)

Fiergola,
North Dakota Century Code 47-01-15: Determining
North Dakota's Interest in the Beds of Navigable
Waters.
59 N.D.L. Rev. 211 (1983)

Smith,
Justice Potter Stewart: A Contemporary Jurist's
View of Religious Liberty.
59 N.D.L. Rev. 183 (1983)

Article III
Powers Reserved To The People

Comment,
Schools - Nature of the Right to Instruction - The
Substantive Requirements of "Free Appropriate
Public Education" Under the Education of All
Handicapped Children Act of 1975.
59 N.D.L. Rev. 629 (1983)

Article IV
Legislative Branch

Comment,
Apportionment in North Dakota: The Saga of
Continuing Controversy.
57 N.D.L. Rev. 447 (1981)

Article VIII
Education

Comment,
Schools - Nature of the Right to Instruction - The
Substantive   Requirements   of   "Free   Appropriate
Public   Education"   Under   the   Education   of   All
Handicapped Children Act of 1975.
59 N.D.L. Rev. 629 (1983)

Article X
Finance and Public Debt

Fiergola,
North   Dakota   Century   Code   ss.   47-01-15:
Determining North Dakota's Interest in the Beds of
Navigable Waters.
59 N.D.L. Rev. 211 (1983)

Article XIII
Compact With United States

Barsh,
Indian Land Claims Policy in the United States.
58 N.D.L. Rev. 7 (1982)

OHIO

Chapter Thirty-five
OHIO CONSTITUTION- 1851

Article I
Bill of Rights

Smith,
"Shall Make No law Abridging..." an Analysis of the
neglected, But Nearly Absolute, Right of Petition.
54 Cin. L. Rev. 1153 (1986)

Sedler,
The State Constitutions and the Supplemental
Protection of Individual Rights.
16 Toledo L. Rev. 465 (1985)

Slovenko,
Symposium: The Legal System and Homosexuality--
Approbation, Accommodation, or Reprobation.
10 U. Dayton L. Rev. 445 (1985)

Williams,
State Constitutional Law in Ohio and the Nation.
16 Toledo L. Rev. 391 (1985)

Comment,
The Writ-Writers: Jailhouse Lawyers' Right of
Meaningful Access to the Courts.
18 Akron L. Rev. 649 (1985)

Comment,
Does the "One-Party Consent" Exception Effectuate
the Underlying Goals of Title III?
18 Akron L. Rev. 495 (1985)

Comment,
Parent--Child Tort Immunity law in Ohio.
18 Akron L. Rev. 667 (1985)

Comment,
State Constitutions' Remedy Guarantee Provisions
Provide More Than Mere "Lip Service" to Rendering
Justice.
16 Toledo L. Rev. 585 (1985)

Comment,
The Public Use Limitation on Eminent Domain After
Hawaii Housing Authority v. Midkiff: Does it Still
Exist?
12 N.Ky. L. Rev. 65 (1985)

Ansell,
Property Versus Civil Rights: An Alternative to the
Double Standard.
11 N.Ky. L. Rev. 51 (1984)

Berger,
Death Penalties and Hugo Bedau: A Crusading
Philosopher Goes Overboard.
45 Ohio St. L.J. 863 (1984)

Browning,
On Privacy, Pen Registers, and State Constitutions:
The Colorado Supreme Court Rejects Smith v.
Maryland.
15 Toledo L. Rev. 1467 (1984)

Fleischaker,
Incursions on Access: "Privacy" Versus the First
Amendment.
15 Toledo L. Rev. 641 (1984)

Goldberg,
Escobedo and Miranda revisited.
14 Akron L. Rev.177 (1984)

Kelly,
Richmond Newspapers and the First Amendment
Right of Access.
18 Akron L. Rev. 33 (1984)

Levine,
Preventing Defense Counsel Error--An Analysis of
Some Ineffective Assistance of Counsel Claims and
their Implication for Professional Regulation.
15 Toledo L. Rev. 1275 (1984)

McCann,
School Board Authority and First Amendment Rights:
The View After Bd. of Educ., Island Trees v. Pico.
18 Akron L. Rev. 283 (1984)

Null,
Municipal Immunity in Ohio--How Much Wrong can
a Municipality do?
15 Toledo L. Rev. 1559 (1984)

Streib,
Capital Punishment of Children in Ohio: "They'd
Never Send a Boy of Seventeen to the Chair in
Ohio, Would They?"
18 Akron L. Rev. 51 (1984)

Comment,
Resolving the Free Exercise and Establishment
Conflict in Caldor v. Thornton: Analysis of
Legislation Designed to Protect Religious Freedom
or Prevent Discrimination.
35 Case W. Res. L. Rev. 132 (1984)

Comment,
The New Breed of Municipal Dog Control Laws:
Are They Constitutional?
53 Cin. L. Rev. 1067 (1984)

Comment,
The Exercise of Supervisory Powers to Dismiss a
Grand Jury Indictment--A Basis for Curbing
Prosecutorial Misconduct.
45 Ohio St. L.J. 1077 (1984)

Comment,
The Ineffective Assistance of Counsel Quandary:
The Debate Continues. Strickland v. Washington.
18 Akron L. Rev. 325 (1984)

Comment,
Public School Searches and the Fourth Amendment.
9 U. Dayton L. Rev. 521 (1984)

Comment,
"Inevitable Discovery" or Inevitable Demise of the
Exclusionary Rule? Nix v. Williams.
18 Akron L. Rev. 309 (1984)

Comment,
South Dakota v. Neville: Blood-Alcohol Test
Refusals and the Fifth Amendment.
11 Ohio N.U.L. Rev. 169 (1984)

Comment,
Seizures of the Fourth Kind: Changing the Rules.
33 Clev. St. L. Rev. 323 (1984)

Comment,
United States v. Leon: The Court Redefines the
Right to the Exclusionary Remedy.
16 Toledo L. Rev. 345 (1984)

Comment,
United States v. Place.   Seizing Luggage on
Reasonable Suspicion--Has Airport Luggage Gone to
the Dogs?
11 Ohio N.U.L. Rev. 417 (1984)

Comment,
A Reconsideration of Proportionality in Sentencing
Procedures: Solem v. Helm.
11 Ohio N.U.L. Rev. 429 (1984)

Comment,
Ohio's New Wrongful Death Statute: An Expanded
Scope of Recoverable Damages.
53 Cin. L. Rev. 1083 (1984)

Comment,
The New Breed of Municipal Dog Control Laws:
Are They Constitutional?
53 Cin. L. Rev. 1067 (1984)

Comment,
Symposium--Statute of Limitations: Discovery Rule
for Malpractice.
17 Akron L. Rev. 655 (1984)

Moore,
Their Life is in the Blood: Jehovah's Witnesses,
Blood Transfusions and the Courts.
10 N.Ky. L. Rev. 281 (1983)

O'Brien,
Driving Under the Influence of Alcohol in Ohio
After Senate Bill 432--The Prosecutor's Viewpoint.
15 Toledo L. Rev. 171 (1983)

Comment,
Robbins, Belton and Ross: Reconsideration of
"Bright Line" Rules for Warrantless Container
Searches.
31 Clev. St. L. Rev. 529 (1983)

Comment,
Can Municipal Immunity in Ohio Be Resurrected
from the Sewers After Haverlack v. Portage Homes,
Inc.?
13 Cap. U.L. Rev. 41 (1983)

Comment,
Book Removal in Secondary Schools--A Violation of
the First Amendment? Board of Education v. Pico.
17 Akron L. Rev. 483 (1983)

Comment,
Free Press--Fair Trial: A Proposal to Extend the
Right of Access to Encompass Pre-Trial Proceedings.
52 Cin. L. Rev. 524 (1983)

Ashman,
Handgun Control by Local Government.
10 N.Ky. L. Rev. 97 (1982)

Gardiner,
To Preserve Liberty--A Look at the Right to Keep
and Bear Arms.
10 N.Ky. L. Rev. 63 (1982)

Gottlieb,
Gun Ownership: A Constitutional Right.
10 N.Ky. L. Rev. 113 (1982)

Halbrook,
To Keep and Bear Their Private Arms: The
Adoption of the Second Amendment, 1787-1791.
10 N.Ky. L. Rev. 13 (1982)

Hennemuth,
Ohio's Last Word on Comparative Negligence?
9 Ohio N.U.L. Rev. 31 (1982)

Comment,
Second Amendment Survey.
10 N.Ky. L. Rev. 155 (1982)

Comment,
Criminal Procedure--Sixth Amendment: The
Admissibility at Trial of Preliminary Hearing
Testimony When the Witness is Unavailable to
Testify.
51 Cin. L. Rev. 171 (1982)

Comment,
Publicly-Funded Display of Religious Symbols: The
Nativity Scene Controversy.
51 Cin. L. Rev. 353 (1982)

Comment,
Widmar v. Vincent: The Protection of Religious
Speech in the Public University.
9 Ohio N.U.L. Rev. 503 (1982)

Comment,
State v. Byrd: Judicial Participation in Plea
Bargaining--Fundamental Fairness?
8 Ohio N.U.L. Rev. 212 (1981)

Comment,
A Foot in the Government's Door--Access Rights of
the Press and Public: Richmond Newspapers, Inc. v.
Virginia.
12 Toledo L. Rev. 991 (1981)

Comment,
The Constitutionality of Student-Initiated Religious
Meetings on Public School Grounds.
50 Cin. L. Rev. 740 (1981)

Koch,
A Further Look at Jago v. Papp: Some Comments
on the Fourth, Fifth and Sixth Amendments.
7 N.Ky. L. Rev. 385 (1980)

Comment,
There is No Exception to the Seventh Amendment
Right to a Jury Trial Based on the Complexity of
Legal and Factual Issues Presented.
49 Cin. L. Rev. 506 (1980)

Comment,
State v. Jackson: Balancing the Right to Confront
with the Admission into Evidence of Preliminary
Hearing Testimony.
10 Cap. U.L. Rev. 365 (1980)

Comment,
Trials   Within   a   Penitentiary--Unconstitutional:
State v. Lane.
9 Cap. U.L. Rev. 795 (1980)

Comment,
Peebles   v.   Clement: Creditors'   Prejudgment
Remedies Under Attack in Ohio.
10 Cap. U.L. Rev. 397 (1980)

Comment,
Education is Not a Fundamental Right and the Ohio
School Funding System is Valid Under Both the
Equal Protection and Thorough and Efficient Clauses
of the Ohio Constitution.
48 Cin. L. Rev. 112 (1979)

Article II
Legislative

Pierce,
The   Regulation   of   Genetic   Testing   in   the
Workplace--a Legislative Proposal.
46 Ohio St. L.J. 771 (1985)

Rosenberg,
Referendum Zoning: Legal Doctrine and Practice.
53 Cin. L. Rev. 381 (1984)

Comment,
Legislative Veto in Ohio: The "Twilight Zone" of
Distinction.
9 U. Dayton L. Rev. 557 (1984)

Comment,
The Current Use of the Initiative and Referendum
in Ohio and Other States.
53 Cin. L. Rev. 541 (1984)

Comment,
The Crumbling Tower of Architectural Immunity:
Evolution and Expansion of the Liability to Third
Parties.
45 Ohio St. L.J. 217 (1984)

Butler,
The Compensability of a Physical Injury as a Result
of Mental Stimulus in Workers' Compensation--The
Dark Ages in Ohio.
13 Cap. U.L. Rev. 1 (1983)

Gough,
Intentional Torts in the Workplace--Further Erosion
of the Workers' Compensation Act Exclusive Remedy
Bar to Tort Actions--Blankenship v. Cincinnati
Milacron Chemicals, Inc.
10 N.Ky. L. Rev. 355 (1983)

O'Brien,
Driving Under the Influence of Alcohol in Ohio
after Senate Bill 432--The Prosecutor's Viewpoint.
15 Toledo L. Rev. 171 (1983)

Comment,
Viers v. Dunlap: Prospective Application of
Comparative Negligence.
10 Ohio N.U.L. Rev. 213 (1983)

Comment,
Ohio's Comparative Negligence Statute: Given
Prospective Application in Viers v. Dunlap.
12 Cap. U.L. Rev. 639 (1983)

Comment,
Workers' Compensation in Ohio: Scope of
Employment and the Intentional Tort.
17 Akron L. Rev. 249 (1983)

Comment,
State ex rel. Berry v. Industrial Commission:
Impact of a New Specificity Requirement in Light of
the Abrogation of the Same Evidence Test.
13 Cap. U.L. Rev. 279 (1983)

Comment,
Blankenship v. Cincinnati Milacron Chemicals, Inc.:
Some Fairness for Ohio Employers.
15 Toledo L. Rev. 403 (1983)

Hennemuth,
Ohio's Last Word on Comparative Negligence?   RC
ss 2315.19.
9 Ohio N.U.L. Rev. 31 (1982)

Knight,
The Need for Workers' Compensation Reform in
Ohio's Definition of Injury: Szymanski v. Halle's
Department Store.
31 Clev. St. L. Rev. 145 (1982)

Wise,
The Retroactive Application of Ohio's Comparative
Negligence Statute--A Golden Opportunity.
9 Ohio N.U.L. Rev. 63 (1982)

Comment,
Blankenship v. Cinti. Milacron Chemical Inc.:
Workers' Compensation and the Intentional Tort; a
New Direction for Ohio.
12 Cap. U.L. Rev. 287 (1982)

Comment,
Ohio Constitution: Initiative and Referendum.
15 Akron L. Rev. 157 (1981)

Comment,
Garcia v. Siffrin: Ohio's Cities May Deny Their
Retarded   Citizens   the   Least   Restrictive   Living
Environment.
11 Cap. U.L. Rev. 111 (1981)

Comment,
Municipal   Corporations-Zoning-Housing-ORC   ss
5123.18(D), (E) and (G), Which Provide for the
Zoning of Group Homes for the Mentally Retarded
Persons in Residential Districts Despite Conflicting
Local   Zoning   Ordinance,   are   Unconstitutional--
Garcia v. Siffrin Residential Ass'n.
50 Cin. L. Rev. 423 (1981)

Comment,
Third Party's Rights Under Ohio's Workmen's [sic]
Compensation System: Will Comparative Negligence
Relieve the Inequities?
11 Cap. U.L. Rev. 285 (1981)

Article IV
Judicial

Comment,
Ohio's Attempt to Halt the Medical Malpractice
Crisis: Effective or Meaningless?
9 U. Dayton L. Rev. 361 (1984)

Devine,
Mandatory   Arbitration   of   Attorney-Client   Fee
Disputes: A Concept Whose Time Has Come.
14 Toledo L. Rev. 1205 (1983)

Comment,
Professional   Corporation   Shareholder   Liability   in
Ohio: Confounding Attorneys and others.   South
High Development Ltd. v. Weiner, Lippe & Cromley
Co., L.P.A.
17 Akron L. Rev. 143 (1983)

Bell,
Symposium: Intermediate Appellate Court Practice-
-Problems and Solutions.
16 Akron L. Rev. 1 (1982)

Davidow,
Judicial Selection: the Search for Quality and
Representativeness.
31 Case W. Res. L. Rev. 409 (1981)

Article VI
Education

Gold,
Public Aid to Private Enterprise Under the Ohio
Constitution: Sections 4, 6, and 13 of Article VIII
in Historical Perspective.
16 Toldeo L.Rev. 405 (1985)

Comment,
Equal Educational Opportunity and Public School
Finance Reform in Ohio: Board of Education v.
Walter.
41 Ohio St. L.J. 179 (1980)

Comment,
The School Funding Challenge in Ohio: Board of
Education v. Walter.
11 Toledo L. Rev. 1019 (1980)

Article VIII
Public Debt and Public Works

Comment,
Public Aid to Private Enterprise Under the Ohio
Constitution: Sections 4, 6 and 13 of Article VIII
in Historical Perspective.
16 Toledo L. Rev. 405 (1985)

Comment,
Revenue Bonds Financing Home Mortgages: Can
This Governmental Role Overcome Constitutional and
Pragmatic Obstacles?
12 Toledo L. Rev. 429 (1981)

Gotherman,
Transition from Village to City Status.
9 Cap. U.L. Rev. 621 (1980)

Article XI
Apportionment

Velde,
One Person-One Vote Round III: Challenges to the
1980 Redistricting.
32 Clev. St. L. Rev. 569 (1984)

Comment,
After H.B. 920:   An Analysis of Needed Real
Property Tax Reform.
30 Clev. St. L. Rev. 137 (1981)

Article XIII
Corporations

Comment,
Professional Corporation Shareholder Liability in
Ohio: Confounding Attorneys and Others. South
High Development Ltd. v. Weiner, Lippe & Cromley
Co., L.P.A.
17 Akron L. Rev. 143 (1983)

Article XVIII
Municipal Corporations

Rodney,
Ohio Municipal Home Rule Re-examined--The Impact
of Garcia v. San Antonio Metropolitan Transit
Authority.
17 U. Dayton L. Rev. 23 (1985)

Comment,
Municipal Home Rule in Ohio: A Mechanism for
Local Regulation of Hazardous Waste Facilities.
16 Toledo L. Rev. 553 (1985)

Comment,
The Municipally Owned Electric Company's
Exemption from Utility Commission Regulation: The
Consumer's Perspective.
33 Case W. Res. L. Rev. 294 (1983)

Bond,
Home Rule--A Revitalized Principle for Noncharter
Municipalities.
54 Ohio B. 1 (1981)

Comment,
Garcia v. Siffrin: Ohio's Cities May Deny Their
Retarded Citizens the Least Restrictive Living
Environment.
11 Cap. U.L. Rev. 111 (1981)

Comment,
<u>Municipal   Corporations-Zoning-Housing-ORC   ss
5123.18(d),   (e)   and   (G),   Which   Provide   for   the
Zoning   of   Group   Homes   for   the   Mentally   Retarded
Persons   in   Residential   Districts   Despite   Conflicting
Local   Zoning   Ordinance,   are   Unconstitutional--
Garcia v. Siffrin Residential Ass'n</u>.
50 Cin. L. Rev. 423 (1981)

OKLAHOMA

Chapter Thirty-six
OKLAHOMA CONSTITUTION- 1907

Preamble

Comment,
Public Land Law: Preemption of State Regulation
of Mineral Development on the Public Domain.
Ventura County v. Gulf Oil Corp.
16 Tulsa L.J. 317 (1980)

Article I
Federal Relations

Cantrell,
Restoring Balance in Federalism.
10 Okla. City U.L. Rev. 1 (1985)

Marshall,
1983 Decisions of Interest Pertaining to Real
Property.
55 Okla. B.J. 699 (1984)

Segreti,
Vesting Whole "Arising Under" Power of District
Courts in Federal Preemption Cases.
37 Okla. L. Rev. 539 (1984)

Comment,
Freedom of Religion and Oklahoma Guardianships:
In re Polin.
19 Tulsa L.J. 668 (1984)

Comment,
Osages, Iron Horses and Reversionary Interests:
Impact of United States v. Atterberry on Railroad
Abandonments.
20 Tulsa L.J. 255 (1984)

Comment,
Taxation: Merrion v. Jicarilla Apache Tribe: Wine
or Vinegar For Oklahoma Tribes?
37 Okla. L. Rev. 369 (1984)

Comment,
Constitutional Law: Religion in Public Schools:
Bender v. Williamsport Area School District.
37 Okla. L. Rev. 327 (1984)

Lester,
Decisions and Actions of 1983 Affecting Federalism.
54 Okla. B.J. 3282 (1983)

Krauss,
Irony of Native American "Rights."
8 Okla. City U.L. Rev. 409 (1983)

Comment,
Rebuilding   Federal   Citadel?   Equal   Employment
Opportunity Commission v. Wyoming.
8 Okla. City U.L. Rev. 551 (1983)

Addicott,
Annulment in Oklahoma.
53 Okla. B.J. 791 (1982)

Lester,
Future of Federalism: Report on Legal and Political
Activities of 1982 as they Affected Federalism and
Their Implications.
53 Okla. B.J. 3079 (1982)

Comment,
Constitutional Law: Widmar v. Vincent: Departure
from   Traditional   Approach   to   Cases   Involving
Religion and Education.
35 Okla. L. Rev. 604 (1982)

Comment,
United States v. Lee: Insensitive Approach to Free
Exercise of Religion.
18 Tulsa L.J. 305 (1982)

Comment,
Creation Science and Balanced Treatment Acts: Examining McLean v. Board of Education and a Modest Predication on Keith v. Department of Education.
7 Okla. City U.L. Rev. 109 (1982)

Comment,
"One Step Beyond": Commerce Clause and Federalism after FERC v. Mississippi.
7 Okla. City U.L. Rev. 243 (1982)

French,
Views of Justice Rehnquist Concerning Proper Role of States in National Labor Relations Policy.
17 Tulsa L.J. 76 (1981)

Gable,
Glimpse at Right to Financial Privacy or "The Bank that Talked Too Much."
52 Okla. B.J. 1565 (1981)

Albert,
Federal Investigation of Video Evangelism: FCC Probes the PTL Club.
33 Okla. L. Rev. 782 (1980)

Blackburn,
Annual Survey of Oklahoma Law: Constitutional Law--Contract Clause.
5 Okla. City U.L. Rev. 153 (1980)

Strickland,
Price of Free man: Resources for Study of Indian law, History, and Policy at University of Tulsa.
15 Tulsa L.J. 720 (1980)

Comment,
Holistic Medicine and Freedom of Religion.
15 Tulsa L.J. 644 (1980)

Comment,
Public Land Law: Preemption of State Regulation of Mineral Development on the Public Domain. Ventura County v. Gulf Oil Corp.
16 Tulsa L.J. 317 (1980)

Comment,
Church vs. State and Supreme Court: Current
Meaning of Establishment Clause.
5 Okla. City U.L. Rev. 683 (1980)

Comment,
American Indian Water Law Symposium.
15 Tulsa L.J. 699 (1980)

Article II
Bill of Rights

Adams,
Service of Process Under Oklahoma Pleading Code.
20 Tulsa L.J. 137 (1984)

Miller,
Oklahoma's Constitutional Right Against Self-
Incrimination and Introduction into Evidence of
Refusal to Take Sobriety Test.
37 Okla. L. Rev. 245 (1984)

Noe,
Tide in Turmoil: Constitutionality of Maritime in
Rem Arrest.
9 Okla. City U.L. Rev. 451 (1984)

Shaw,
Corporate Political Speech and First Amendment.
9 Okla. City U.L. Rev. 271 (1984)

Comment,
Constitutionality of Drunk Drive Roadblocks in
Oklahoma: State v. Smith.
20 Tulsa L.J. 286 (1984)

Comment,
Fourth Amendment Warrants Clause--Totality of
Circumstances Test and Good Faith Exception After
Illinois v. Gates.
9 Okla. City U.L. Rev. 175 (1984)

Comment,
Illinois v. Gates: Abandonment of Aguilar-
Spinnelli.
9 Okla. City U.L. Rev. 355 (1984)

Cronin,
Plain View and Party Balloons.
8 Okla. City U.L. Rev. 161 (1983)

Dowlut,
Right to Arms: Does Constitution or Predilection of Judges Reign?
36 Okla. L. Rev. 65 (1983)

Trubitt,
Patchwork Verdicts, Different-Jurors Verdicts, and American Jury Theory: Whether Verdicts are Invalidated by Juror Disagreement on Issues.
36 Okla. L. Rev. 473 (1983)

Comment,
Oklahoma's Plain View Rule: Licensing Unreasonable Searches and Seizures?
18 Tulsa L.J. 674 (1983)

Comment,
Criminal Law: Oregon v. Kennedy: Avoiding Double Jeopardy Bar.
36 Okla. L. Rev. 697 (1983)

Comment,
Criminal Procedure: Oklahoma's Motion for New Trial in Criminal Cases.
36 Okla. L. Rev. 888 (1983)

Comment,
Restricting Availability of Federal Habeas Corpus: Lehman v. Lycoming County Children's Services.
19 Tulsa L.J. 118 (1983)

Comment,
Constitutional Law: Equal Protection Clause: Effect of Plyler v. Doe on Intermediate Scrutiny.
36 Okla. L. Rev. 321 (1983)

Cornish,
Where have all the Children Gone?--Reverse Certification.
35 Okla. L. Rev. 373 (1982)

Dowlut,
State Constitutions and Rights to Keep and Bear
Arms.
7 Okla. City U.L. Rev. 177 (1982)

Hunt,
Oil & Gas: Retroactive Application of Oklahoma's
Statutory Pugh Clause?
53 Okla. B.J. 487 (1982)

Jordan,
Evaluating Admissibility of Testimony of Previously
Hypnotized Witnesses.
53 Okla. B.J. 1023 (1982)

Minnis,
Civil Discovery in Oklahoma Revisited Under New
Code.
18 Tulsa L.J. 173 (1982)

Sherman,
Child Custody Jurisdiction and Parental Kidnapping
Prevention Act--Due Process Dilemma?
17 Tulsa L.J. 713 (1982)

Taylor,
Landowners' Equitable Remedies Under Article II,
Section 24 Oklahoma Constitution.
55 Okla. B.J. 501 (1982)

Comment,
Criminal Procedure: Sufficiency of Trial Judge's
Findings on Voluntariness of Confession.
35 Okla. L. Rev. 807 (1982)

Comment,
United States v. Ross: Comparison with Major
Automobile Exception Cases.
7 Okla. City U.L. Rev. 77 (1982)

Comment,
New Rules for Open Courts: Progress or Empty
Promise?
18 Tulsa L.J. 147 (1982)

Comment,
Legislation: Oklahoma's   Statutory   Definition   of
Death.
35 Okla. L. Rev. 615 (1982)

Barrett,
Annual   Survey   of   Oklahoma   Law: Constitutional
Law--Equal   Protection: Unilateral   Award   of
Attorney's Fees.
6 Okla. City U.L. Rev. 583 (1981)

Barrett,
Constitutional   Law--Due   Process: Mechanics'   and
Materialmen's Lien Statutes.
6 Okla. City U.L. Rev. 575 (1981)

Cordell,
Police   Inventory   of   Impounded   Vehicles--Searching
for Standard.
52 Okla. B.J. 3058 (1981)

Gable,
Glimpse   at   Right   to   Financial   Privacy   or   "The   Bank
that Talked Too Much."
52 Okla. B.J. 1565 (1981)

Grissom,
Annual   Survey   of   Oklahoma   Law: Criminal   Law   and
Procedure--Indictments and Informations.
6 Okla. City U.L. Rev. 84 (1981)

Hill,
We Only Promised you a "Weingarten."
6 Okla. City U.L. Rev. 395 (1981)

Ingram and Domph,
Right to Govern One's Personal Appearance.
6 Okla. City U.L. Rev. 339 (1981)

Jones,
Criminal   Law   and   Procedure--Denial   or   Revocation
of Bail for Purpose of Pretrial Preventive Detention.
6 Okla. City U.L. Rev. 130 (1981)

Jones,
Annual Survey of Oklahoma Law: Criminal Law and
Procedure--Denial or Revocation of Bail for Purpose
or Pretrial Preventive Detention.
6 Okla. City U.L. Rev. 130 (1981)

Mattson,
Pregnancy Amendment: Unanswered Question of
Employer Responsibility for Fetal Rights.
52 Okla. B.J. 1232 (1981)

Musser,
1980 Decisions of Interest Pertaining to Real
Property.
52 Okla. B.J. 429 (1981)

Nelson,
Media Defamation in Oklahoma: Modest Proposal
and New Perspectives--Part I.
34 Okla. L. Rev. 478 (1981)

Nelson,
Media Defamation in Oklahoma: Modest Proposal
and New Perspectives--Part II.
34 Okla. L. Rev. 737 (1981)

Plourde,
Criminal Law and Procedure--Right to Speedy Trial.
6 Okla. City U.L. Rev. 126 (1981)

Plourde,
Eyewitness Identification Testimony.
6 Okla. City U.L. Rev. 632 (1981)

Plourde,
Right to Proceed Pro Se.
6 Okla. City U.L. Rev. 121 (1981)

Prentice,
Consolidated Edison and Bellotti: First Amendment
Protection of Corporate Political Speech.
16 Tulsa L.J. 599 (1981)

Ranhal,
Mental Patients' Constitutional Right to Refuse
Treatment.
6 Okla. City U.L. Rev. 45 (1981)

Richardson,
When is State Estopped From Prosecuting Defendant
at Two (or more) Trials for Crimes Arising From
Single-Episode?
52 Okla. B.J. 947 (1981)

Spector,
State Sovereign Immunity in Tort: Oklahoma's Long
and Tortuous Road.
34 Okla. L. Rev. 526 (1981)

Tucker,
Torts--Right of Privacy.
6 Okla. City U.L. Rev. 299 (1981)

Vines,
Criminal Law and Procedure--Right to Unanimous
Verdict from Six-Member Juries.
6 Okla. City U.L. Rev. 620 (1981)

Comment,
Criminal Procedure: Good Faith Exception to
Exclusionary Rule.
34 Okla. L. Rev. 197 (1981)

Comment,
Municipal Corporations: Recommended Procedure
for "Accelerating" or "Revoking" Continued
Sentences.
34 Okla. L. Rev. 152 (1981)

Comment,
Constitutionality of Oklahoma's Prohibition on
Liquor Advertising.
16 Tulsa L.J. 734 (1981)

Comment,
Constitutional Law: Death Penalty: Critique of
Philosophical Bases Held to Satisfy Eighth
Amendment Requirements for its Justification.
34 Okla. L. Rev. 567 (1981)

Comment,
Inconsistent Due Process Standards Applied to Cases
of Exclusion From Educational Institutions.
34 Okla. L. Rev. 291 (1981)

Comment,
Constitutional Law: Search and Seizure: Analysis
of Federal and Oklahoma Law in Light of Recent
Chicago Strip Search Cases.
34 Okla. L. Rev. 312 (1981)

Comment,
County of Washington v. Gunther: Movement
Towards Comparable Worth?
17 Tulsa L.J. 327 (1981)

Adams,
Civil Discovery in Oklahoma: General Principles.
16 Tulsa L.J. 184 (1980)

Anastasiadis,
Collateral Estoppel and/or Double Jeopardy: Bar to
Probation Revocation Using Same Evidence After
Defendant Has Been Acquitted of Criminal Charges
that Form Basis for Revocation.
51 Okla. B.J. 3079 (1980)

Anderson,
Indian Employment Preference: Legal Foundations
and Limitations.
15 Tulsa L.J. 733 (1980)

Barnes,
Constitutional Law--Due Process.
5 Okla. City U.L. Rev. 135 (1980)

Cox,
Application of "Sunset" Principles to State Judicial
Functions: Judges as Fact Finders.
33 Okla. L. Rev. 681 (1980)

Dunagan,
Overview of Pre-Trial Preparation for Business
Related Litigation.
16 Tulsa L.J. 139 (1980)

Gray,
Juvenile Law--Juvenile Matters in General.
5 Okla. City U.L. Rev. 259 (1980)

Hurd,
Evidence--Evidentiary harpoons.
5 Okla. City U.L. Rev. 223 (1980)

LeFrancoi,
Constitution and "Right" to Marry: Jurisprudential
Analysis.
5 Okla. City U.L. Rev. 507 (1980)

Miller,
New Rule Effective Assistance of Counsel and
Exception.
51 Okla. B.J. 3103 (1980)

Murrah,
Application of Sullivan and its Progeny to Public
Defamation Actions in Oklahoma.
51 Okla. B.J. 3073 (1980)

Spector,
Swords, Shields, and Quest for Truth in Trial
Process: Road from Constitutional Standards to
Evidentiary Havens.
33 Okla. L. Rev. 520 (1980)

Zwiebel,
Informed Right to Self-Representation.
5 Okla. City U.L. Rev. 199 (1980)

Zwiebel,
Criminal Law and Procedure In-Court Identification.
5 Okla. City U.L. Rev. 202 (1980)

Comment,
Civil Rights: Liability of Private Coconspirator
under 42 U.S.C. ss 1983 When Acting in Conspiracy
with Immune State Judge.
33 Okla. L. Rev. 824 (1980)

Comment,
No-Spouse Employment Policy as Constituting
Marital Discrimination.
33 Okla. L. Rev. 636 (1980)

Comment,
Constitutional Law: Summary Revocation of
Involuntary Mental Patient's Convalescent Leave--
Is it Unconstitutional?
33 Okla. L. Rev. 366 (1980)

Comment,
Criminal law: Oklahoma's Death Penalty Statutes
Reviewed.
33 Okla. L. Rev. 448 (1980)

Article III
Suffrage

Arrow,
Dimensions of Newly Emergent, Quasi-Fundamental
Right to Political Candidacy.
6 Okla. City U.L. Rev. 1 (1981)

Article IV
Distribution of Powers

Clark,
Annual Survey of Oklahoma Law: legal Profession--
Residency Not Required for Active Bar Members to
practice Law in Oklahoma.
6 Okla. City U.L. Rev. 236 (1981)

Cox,
State   Judicial   Power: Separation   of   Powers
Perspective.
34 Okla. L. Rev. 207 (1981)

Article V
Legislative Department

Minnis,
Washington   Update: Legislation   and   Issues   of
Interest.
53 Okla. B.J. 509 (1982)

Cox,
State   Judicial   Power: Separation   of   Powers
Perspective.
34 Okla. L. Rev. 207 (1981)

Ferrandino,
Annual Survey of Oklahoma Law: Elections--Taking
"Initiative" in Oklahoma.
6 Okla. City U.L. Rev. 673 (1981)

Kaplan,
Annual Survey of Oklahoma Law: Constitutional
law--State Constitution.
6 Okla. City U.L. Rev. 589 (1981)

Rueb,
Annual Survey of Oklahoma Law: Ad Valorem Tax.
5 Okla. City U.L. Rev. 336 (1980)

Article VI
Executive Department

Cox,
State   Judicial   Power: Separation   of   Powers
Perspective.
34 Okla. L. Rev. 207 (1981)

Comment,
Constitutional Law: Impact of Branti v. Finkel on
Political Patronage Employment.
34 Okla. L. Rev. 93 (1981)

Cox,
Application of "Sunset" Principles to State Judicial
Functions: Judges as Fact Finders.
33 Okla. L. Rev. 681 (1980)

Article VII
Judicial Department

Segreti,
Vesting Whole "Arising Under" Power of District
Courts in Federal Preemption Cases.
37 Okla. L. Rev. 539 (1984)

Melson,
Judicial Reform in Oklahoma Trial Courts: Two
Proposals.
54 Okla. B.J. 1409 (1983)

Comment,
Restricting Availability of Federal habeas Corpus:
Lehman v. Lycoming County Children's Services.
19 Tulsa L.J. 118 (1983)

Hargrave,
Brief Observations on Appealable Orders.
53 Okla. B.J. 1015 (1982)

Cook,
Annual Survey of Oklahoma Law: Pleading and
Procedure--Remedies: Mandamus and Prohibition in
Supreme Court.
6 Okla. City U.L. Rev. 788 (1981)

Golden,
Annual Survey of Oklahoma Law: legal Profession--
Residency Not Required for Active Bar Members to
practice in Oklahoma.
6 Okla. City U.L. Rev. 236 (1981)

Comment,
Administrative Law: Primary Jurisdiction in Stipe v.
Theus?
34 Okla. L. Rev. 86 (1981)

Owens,
Annual Survey of Oklahoma Law: Civil Pleadings
and Procedure--Proper Use of Order Nunc Pro Tunc.
5 Okla. City U.L. Rev. 102 (1980)

Rahnal,
Annual Survey of Oklahoma Law: Subject Matter
Jurisdiction.
5 Okla. City U.L. Rev. 72 (1980)

Article VII-A
Court on the Judiciary

Maseth,
Annual Survey of Oklahoma Law: Professional
Responsibility--Judicial   Misconduct--Grounds   for
Attorney Discipline.
5 Okla. City U.L. Rev. 293 (1980)

Article IX
Corporations

Comment,
Osages, Iron Horses and Reversionary Interest:
Impact of United States v. Atterberry on Railroad
Abandonments.
20 Tulsa L.J. 255 (1984)

Comment,
Subject Matter Jurisdiction of Oklahoma Corporation
Commission: Tenneco Oil Co. v. El Paso Natural
Gas Co.
19 Tulsa L.J. 465 (1984)

Comment,
Oil and Gas: Ability of the Oklahoma Corporation
Commission to Interpret its Own Orders.
36 Okla. L. Rev. 467 (1983)

Comment,
Public Utilities: Black Fox Nuclear Project
Cancellation Dilemma: Of Judicial Review and
Reform of Oklahoma's Administrative Process.
36 Okla. L. Rev. 190 (1983)

Comment,
Interpretation of Corporation Commission Orders:
Dichotomous Court/Agency Jurisdiction.
8 Okla. City U.L. Rev. 311 (1983)

Comment,
Public Utilities: Reducing the Burden of Nuclear
Power Plant Abandonment.
36 Okla. L. Rev. 176 (1983)

Hargrave,
Brief Observations on Appealable Orders.
53 Okla. B.J. 1015 (1982)

Mogel,
Ratemaking for Oil Pipelines in Outer Continental
Shelf.
17 Tulsa L.J. 469 (1982)

O'Roke,
Public Utility Securities Regulation: New Life for
Old law?
7 Okla. City U.L. Rev. 271 (1982)

Clark,
Annual Survey of Oklahoma Law: Administrative
Law--Public Utility Regulation.
6 Okla. City U.L. Rev. 35 (1981)

Musser,
1980 Decisions of Interest Pertaining to Real
Property.
52 Okla. B.J. 429 (1981)

Prentice,
Consolidated Edison and Bellotti: First Amendment
Protection of Corporate Political Speech.
16 Tulsa L.J. 599 (1981)

Comment,
Corporations: Alien Corporations that Domesticate
in Oklahoma May Hold Land.
34 Okla. L. Rev. 194 (1981)

Rueb,
Annual Survey of Oklahoma Law: Income Tax--
Statutory and Case Law Developments.
5 Okla. City U.L. Rev. 321 (1980)

Article X
Revenue and Taxation

Arnold,
Public Trusts in Oklahoma.
19 Tulsa L.J. 192 (1983)

Musser,
1980 Decisions of Interest Pertaining to Real
Property.
52 Okla. B.J. 429 (1981)

Comment,
Annual Survey of Oklahoma Law: Constitutional
Law--State Constitution.
6 Okla. City U.L. Rev. 589 (1981)

Greenley,
Business Valuations.
16 Tulsa L.J. 41 (1980)

Rueb,
Annual Survey of Oklahoma Law: Ad Valorem Tax.
5 Okla. City U.L. Rev. 336 (1980)

Article XII-A
Homestead Exemption from Taxation

Comment,
Creation   Science   and   Balanced   Treatment   Acts:
Examining   McLean   v.   Board   of   Education   and   a
Modest   Prediction   on   Keith   v.   Department   of
Education.
7 Okla. City U.L. Rev. 109 (1982)

Article XIV
Banks and Banking

Comment,
Alternative   Mortgage   Instruments: Oklahoma
Experience.
8 Okla. City U.L. Rev. 121 (1983)

Comment,
Real Property: usurious Interest Rates In Oklahoma
Real Estate Transactions.
34 Okla. L. Rev. 184 (1981)

Article XVII
Counties

Comment,
Annual Survey of Oklahoma Law: Constitutional
Law--State Constitution.
6 Okla. City U.L. Rev. 589 (1981)

Article XVIII
Municipal Corporations

Arnold,
Public Trusts in Oklahoma.
19 Tulsa L.J. 192 (1983)

Lester,
Municipal Antitrust Liability After Boulder.
36 Okla. L. Rev. 827 (1983)

Article XXI
Public Institutions

Comment,
Annual Survey of Oklahoma Law: Constitutional
Law--State Constitution.
6 Okla. City U.L. Rev. 589 (1981)

Article XXII
Alien and Corporate Ownership of Lands

Musser,
1981 Decisions of Interest Pertinent to Real
Property.
53 Okla. B.J. 501 (1982)

Comment,
Corporations: Alien Corporations that Domesticate
in Oklahoma May Hold Land.
34 Okla. L. Rev. 194 (1981)

Article XXIII
Miscellaneous

Comment,
Setting Standards for Sufficiency of Assumption of
Risk Defense in Oklahoma Manufacturers' Products
Liability Actions: Bingham v. Hollingsworth.
8 Okla. City U.L. Rev. 45 (1983)

Manning,
Annual Survey of Oklahoma Law: Torts--
Manufacturers' Products Liability.
5 Okla. City U.L. Rev. 345 (1980)

Article XXIV
Constitutional Amendments

Ferrandino,
Elections--Taking The "Initiative" In Oklahoma.
6 Okla. City U.L. Rev. 677 (1981)

Article XXV
Social Security

Comment,
Rights of Handicapped in Professional Training
Programs Under ss 504 of Vocational Rehabilitation
Act.
33 Okla. L. Rev. 409 (1980)

OREGON

Chapter Thirty-seven
OREGON CONSTITUTION- 1857

Article I
Bill of Rights

Schuman,
Oregon's Remedy Guarantee: Article I, Section 10
of the Oregon Constitution.
65 Or. L. Rev. 35 (1986)

Waldo,
The 1984 Oregon Death Penalty Initiatives: A State
Constitutional Analysis.
22 Willamette L. Rev. 287 (1986)

Falk,
Delegated Power to Amend Medical Staff Bylaws.
21 Willamette L. Rev. (1985)

Simmons,
Salem College & Academy v. Employment Division:
State   Unemployment   Tax   and   the
Interdenominational School - The Lions Win Again.
21 Willamette L. Rev. 937 (1985)

Comment,
Religious Community As a City: The Oregon
Constitutional Puzzle of State of Oregon v. City of
Rajneeshpuram.
21 Willamette L. Rev. 707 (1985)

Hemphill,
Challenging Conditions of Confinement: A State
Constitutional Approach.
20 Willamette L. Rev. 409 (1984)

Moore,
Oregon's Paramilitary Activities Statute: A Sneak
Attack on the First Amendment.
20 Willamette L. Rev. 335 (1984)

Torno,
Coercion and Free Speech in Oregon: 1983
Legislative Session's Response to State v. Robertson.
20 Willamette L. Rev. 351 (1984)

Wildman,
The Legitimation of Sex Discrimination: A Critical
Response to Supreme Court Jurisprudence.
63 Or. L. Rev. 265 (1984)

Comment,
State Constitutional Analysis of Equal Protection
and Privileges or Immunities: Gender Discrimination
in Oregon.
19 Willamette L. Rev. 757 (1983)

Willner,
Constitutional Interpretation In a Pioneer and
Populist State.
17 Willamette L. Rev. 757 (1981)

Comment,
Suspect's Right to Reconsider Waiver of Assistance
of Counsel Upon the Appearance of an Attorney:
State v. Haynes.
17 Willamette L. Rev. 515 (1981)

Comment,
State Ex Rel. Oregonian Publishing Co. v. Diez: An
End to Soft-Hearted Mollycoddling?
17 Willamette L. Rev. 719 (1981)

Morgan and Shonkwiler,
Regulatory Takings in Oregon: A Walk Down Fifth
Avenue Without Due Process.
16 Willamette L. Rev. 591 (1980)

Article IV
Legislative Department

Etter,
County Home Rule in Oregon Reaches Majority.
61 Or. L. Rev. 3 (1982)

Article IX
Finance

Comment,
Tax   Increment   Financing   for   Development   and
Redevelopment.
61 Or. L. Rev. 123 (1982)

PENNSYLVANIA

Chapter Thirty-eight
PENNSYLVANIA CONSTITUTION- 1874

Article I
Declaration of Rights

Miller,
Discrimination by Gender in Automobile Insurance.
23 Duq. L. Rev. 621 (1985)

Alschuler,
Bright Line Fever and the Fourth Amendment.
45 U. Pitt. L. Rev. 277 (1984)

Lasson,
Group Libel Versus Free Speech: When Big Brother
Should Butt In.
23 Duq. L. Rev. 77 (1984)

Ledewitz,
Pennsylvania Law: the State Constitution Assumes
New Importance.
7 Pa. L.J.-Rep. 1 (1984)

Schreiber,
First   Amendment   Protects   Government   Employees'
Right to Speak on Matters of Public Importance.
57 Tem. L.Q. 301 (1984)

Stango,
Defendant   Charged   With   Possessory   Crime   Has
Automatic Standing Under State Constitution.
57 Tem. L.Q. 343 (1984)

Comment,
Historic   Preservation   Cases   in   Pennsylvania: A
Survey and Analysis.
22 Duq. L. Rev. 22 (1984)

Comment,
Trial Court Must Consider the Public's Right of
Access to a Preliminary Hearing Before Ordering
Closure.
23 Duq. L. Rev. 293 (1984)

Baker,
Outcome Equality or Equality of Respect:
Substantive Content of Equal Protection.
131 U. Pa. L. Rev. 933 (1983)

Comment,
Evidence Seized Pursuant to a Search Warrant
Which Contains Both Valid and Invalid Clauses May
Result in Severance of the Warrant in Order to
Suppress Only that Evidence Seized Pursuant to the
Invalid Clauses.
22 Duq. L. Rev. 231 (1983)

Comment,
Obscenity, Cable Television and the First
Amendment: Will FCC Regulation Impair the
Marketplace of Ideas?
21 Duq. L. Rev. 965 (1983)

Baker,
Corporate Political Expenditures.
130 U. Pa. L. Rev. 646 (1982)

Harper,
Has the Pennsylvania Superior Court Misread Terry
& Adams?
20 Duq. L. Rev. 585 (1982)

LaFave,
Fourth Amendment in an Imperfect World.
43 U.Pitt. L. Rev. 307 (1982)

Kuritz,
"Good Faith" Exception to the Exclusionary Rule.
27 Vill. L. Rev. 211 (1982)

Medow,
First Amendment and the Secrecy State: Snepp v.
United States.
130 U. Pa. L. Rev. 775 (1982)

Phillips,
Neutrality and Purposiveness in the Application of
Strict Scrutiny to Racial Classifications.
55 Tem. L.Q. 317 (1982)

Redish,
Self-Realization, Democracy, and Freedom of
Expression: A Reply to Professor Baker.
130 U. Pa. L. Rev. 678 (1982)

Redish,
Value of Free Speech.
130 U. Pa. L. Rev. 591 (1982)

Seidelson,
Confrontation Clause, the Right Against Self-
Incrimination and the Supreme Court.
20 Duq. L. Rev. 429 (1982)

Comment,
The United States Supreme Court Has Held That
Enactment of a Male-Only Draft Registration
Requirement Does Not Violate The Equal Protection
Component of the Fifth Amendment Due Process
Clause.
20 Duq. L. Rev. 519 (1982)

Comment,
Hypnotically-Refreshed Testimony Admissible,
Subject to Strict Standards Including Procedural
Safeguards.
55 Tem. L.Q. 489 (1982)

Comment,
Excessive Bail Clause of the Eighth Amendment is
Applicable to the States.
20 Duq. L. Rev. 689 (1982)

Comment,
Reconciling The Conflict Between a Proprietary
Interest of the Plaintiff and the Constitutional
Guarantee of Free Speech.
27 Vill. L. Rev. 1205 (1981-1982)

Cramer,
Stopping of Automobile or Arrest of Driver of
Motor Vehicle for Ordinary Traffic Offense Does
Not Without More, Permit Warrantless Search of
Automobile.
54 Tem. L.Q. 527 (1981)

Galie,
The Pennsylvania Constitution and the Protection of
Defendant's Rights, 1969-1980: A Survey.
42 U. Pitt. L. Rev. 269 (1981)

Strazzella,
Commonwealth Appeals and Double Jeopardy.
4 Pa. L.J. 11 (1981)

Comment,
Silence of Accused, No Adverse Interest Instruction.
20 Duq. L. Rev. 71 (1981)

Comment,
Impeachment Use of Prearrest Silence.
54 Tem. L.Q. 331 (1981)

Connors,
Pennsylvania   Constitution   Requires   an   Explicit
Waiver of Miranda Rights.
26 Vill. L. Rev. 205 (1980-81)

Lincicorne,
Governmental Appeal of Criminal Sentence is Not
Unconstitutional as Violative of the Double Jeopardy
Clause.
26 Vill. L. Rev. 1021 (1980-1981)

Comment,
The Propriety of Granting Summary Judgment for
Defendants in Defamation Suits Involving Actual
Malice.
26 Vill. L. Rev. 470 (1980-1981)

Comment,
Right to Counsel During Court-Ordered Psychiatric
Examinations of Criminal Defendants.
26 Vill. L. Rev. 135 (1980-81)

Comment,
Miranda Warnings to Armed Suspect Who Has
Barricaded Himself.
26 Vill. L. Rev. 682 (1980-81)

Arnold,
Right to Trial by Jury in Complex Litigation
Historical Inquiry.
128 U. Pa. L. Rev. 829 (1980)

Gottlieb,
Government Allocation of First Amendment
Resources.
41 U. Pitt. L. Rev. 205 (1980)

Kahana,
Prosecution for Additional Criminal Activity Not
Specified in Original Indictment.
25 Vill. L. Rev. 365 (1980)

Schlesinger,
Exclusionary Rule in Search of a Rationale.
18 Duq. L. Rev. 225 (1980)

Schulhofer,
Due Process, Sentencing.
128 U. Pa. L. Rev. 733 (1980)

Stango,
The Jury Size Question in Pennsylvania: Six of One
and a Dozen of the Other.
53 Tem. L.Q. 89 (1980)

Tanford,
Rape Victim Shield Laws and the Sixth Amendment.
128 U. Pa. L. Rev. 544 (1980)

Comment,
Pennsylvania Obscenity Law: A Pornographer's
Delight.
41 U.Pitt. L. Rev. 251 (1980)

Comment,
Regulating Indecent Speech: A New Attack on the
First Amendment.
41 U. Pitt. L. Rev. 321 (1980)

Comment,
Collateral Estoppel and Federal Litigation Following
a State Court Decision, Search and Seizure.
25 Vill. L. Rev. 403 (1980)

Comment,
Prohibition   of   Group-Based   Stereotypes   in   Jury
Selection Procedures.
25 Vill. L. Rev. 339 (1980)

Comment,
Pennsylvania   Obscenity   Law: A   Pornographer's
Delight.
41 U.Pitt. L. Rev. 251 (1980)

Comment,
Regulating Indecent Speech: A New Attack on the
First Amendment.
41 U. Pitt. L. Rev. 321 (1980)

Comment,
Electronic Surveillance--Covert Entry.
18 Duq. L. Rev. 351 (1980)

Comment,
Searches   by   Drug   Detection   Dogs   in   Pennsylvania
Public Schools.
85 Dick. L. Rev. 143 (1980)

Comment,
Indigent   Criminal   Defendants--Right   to   Assigned
Counsel for Misdemeanors.
18 Duq. L. Rev. 307 (1980)

Comment,
Right to Counsel Retreats.
41 U. Pitt. L. Rev. 647 (1980)

Comment,
Waiver of the Right to Counsel.
18 Duq. L. Rev. 999 (1980)

Article V
The Judiciary

Greenberg,
State Supreme Court Cannot Compel Production of
Judicial Inquiry and Review Board's Confidential
Records.
57 Tem. L.Q. 407 (1984)

Pomeroy,
Foreword: The Pennsylvania Supreme Court in its
First Decade Under the New Judiciary Article.
53 Tem. L.Q. 613 (1980)

Comment,
This Section Compelling State Judges to Retire at
Age 70 Does Not Deny Equal Protection or Due
Process of Law.
54 Tem. L.Q. 375 (1981)

Comment,
Judicial Discipline--Does It Exist in Pennsylvania?
84 Dick. L. Rev. 447 (1980)

Article VIII
Taxation and Finance

Comment,
Agricultural Land Preservation: Can Pennsylvania
Save the Family Farm?
87 Dick. L. Rev. 595 (1983)

Comment,
Tax: Option Granted Domestic Corporations but not
Foreign Corporations for Purposes of Calculating
Capital Stock Tax Held Unconstitutional.
56 Tem. L.Q. 867 (1983)

Ginsberg,
Real Property Tax Exemption of Nonprofit
Organizations.
53 Tem. L.Q. 291 (1980)

Comment,
Tax Exemptions for Educational Institutions:
Discretion and Discrimination.
128 U. Pa. L. Rev. 849 (1980)

RHODE ISLAND

Chapter Thirty-nine
RHODE ISLAND CONSTITUTION- 1986

Article I
Declaration of Certain Constitutional
Rights and Principles

Comment,
Constitution of the State of Rhode Island and
Providence Plantations.
35 R.I. B.J. 22(8) (1987)

Conley,
Civil Rights and Civil Wrongs in Rhode Island:
Church, State and the Constitution 1636-1986.
35 R.I. B.J. 14(9) (1987)

Conley,
Speaking Out: The 1985 State Constitutional
Convention: the Salient Issues.
33 R.I. B.J. 10 (1985)

Article XIV
Constitutional Amendments and Revisions

DiBiase,
Reviving Rhode Island State Constitutional Rights:
The Need for a New Approach to Constitutional
Questions.
35 R.I. B.J. 5(8) (1987)

Comment,
Constitution of the State of Rhode Island and
Providence Plantations.
35 R.I. B.J. 22(8) (1987)

Conley,
Speaking Out: The 1985 State Constitutional
Convention: the Salient Issues.
33 R.I. B.J. 10 (1985)

SOUTH CAROLINA

Chapter Forty
SOUTH CAROLINA CONSTITUTION- 1895

Article I
Declaration of Rights

Grimball,
1981 Survey: State and Local Government; Taxing
Power of an Appointed Body.
34 S.C.L. Rev. 203 (1982)

Hare,
Annual Survey of South Carolina Law: Criminal
Law: Misprision of a Felony.
33 S.C.L. Rev. 65 (1981)

Hare,
Annual Survey of South Carolina Law: Criminal
Law: Waiver of the Double Jeopardy Claim.
33 S.C.L. Rev. 61 (1981)

Zeigler,
Annual   Survey   of   South   Carolina   Law:
Constitutional Law: Separation of Powers.
33 S.C.L. Rev. 25 (1981)

Horres,
Annual   Survey   of   South   Carolina   Law:
Constitutional Law; Equal Protection--the Guest
Statute.
32 S.C.L. Rev. 29 (1980)

Article III
Legislative Department

Quirk,
Taxpayer Remedies in South Carolina.
37 S.C.L. Rev. 489 (1986)

Zeigler,
Annual   Survey   of   South   Carolina   Law:
Constitutional Law: Separation of Powers.
33 S.C.L. Rev. 25 (1981)

Article V
Judicial Department

Zeigler,
Annual   Survey   of   South   Carolina   Law:
Constitutional Law: Separation of Powers.
33 S.C.L. Rev. 25 (1981)

Article VIII
Local Government

Neal,
1982 Survey: State and Local Government;   Home
Rule.
35 S.C.L. Rev. 151 (1983)

Quirk,
Nature of a Business License Tax.
32 S.C.L. Rev. 471 (1981)

Article X
Finance, Taxation and Bonded Debt

Quirk,
Taxpayer Remedies in South Carolina.
37 S.C.L. Rev. 489 (1986)

Devlin,
1981 Survey: State and Local Government;   General
Obligation Bonds and Industrial Revenue Bonds.
34 S.C.L. Rev. 209 (1982)

Quirk,
Nature of a Business License Tax.
32 S.C.L. Rev. 471 (1981)

Article XVII
Miscellaneous Matters

Chastain and Woodside,
Determination of Property Rights Upon Divorce in
South Carolina: An   Exploration   and
Recommendation.
33 S.C.L. Rev. 227 (1981)

Zeigler,
Annual   Survey   of   South   Carolina   Law:
Constitutional Law: Separation of Powers.
33 S.C.L. Rev. 25 (1981)

SOUTH DAKOTA

Chapter Forty-one
SOUTH DAKOTA CONSTITUTION- 1889

Article III
Legislative Department

Lowe,
Restrictions on Initiative and Referendum Powers in
South Dakota.
28 S.D.L. Rev. 53 (1982)

Comment,
Sovereign Immunity and the South Dakota Plaintiff:
A Practical Approach.
26 S.D.L. Rev. 300 (1981)

Smyser,
Constitutional Limitations on the Enactment of
Statutes in South Dakota.
25 S.D.L. Rev. 14 (1980)

Article V
Judicial Department

Hall,
The Unified Judicial System in South Dakota: A
Fifth Year Report.
25 S.D.L. Rev. 1 (1980)

Article VI
Bill of Rights

Comment,
United States v. Leon: Adoption of the Good Faith
Exception to the Exclusionary Rule.
30 S.D.L. Rev. 168 (1984)

Comment,
The American Indian Religious Freedom Act - An
Answer to the Indian's Prayers.
29 S.D.L. Rev. 131 (1983)

Comment,
City of Rapid City v. Kahler: Introducing South
Dakota to the Mire of "Religious Use" in Zoning.
29 S.D.L. Rev. 156 (1983)

Comment,
The Contempt Statutes: At Odds with Domestic
Enforcement?
29 S.D.L. Rev. 164 (1983)

Comment,
Reversion of Railroad Right of Way in South Dakota
After Haack v. Burlington Northern, Inc.
28 S.D.L. Rev. 196 (1982)

Comment,
Chokecherry Hills Estates, Inc. v. Deuel County:
Protection of South Dakota Ecology Through the
Police Power.
26 S.D.L. Rev. 384 (1981)

Article VIII
Education and School Lands

McCindy,
South Dakota Property Rights, Uranium Mining, and
the Use of the Zoning Ordinance as a Means of
Protection.
26 S.D.L. Rev. 206 (1981)

Article XI
Revenue and Finance

Froehlich,
South Dakota Real Property Tax Exemptions: Time
for a Legislative Review.
27 S.D.L. Rev. 1 (1981)

Article XXI
Miscellaneous

Dugan,
Mechanic's Liens for Improvements on Real
Property.
25 S.D.L. Rev. 238 (1980)

Article XXII
Compact with the United States

LaFave,
South Dakota's Forced Fee Indian Land Claims:
Will Landowners be Liable for Government's
Wrongdoing?
30 S.D.L. Rev. 59 (1984)

Clinton,
State Power Over Indian Reservations: A Critical
Comment on Burger Court Doctrine.
26 S.D.L. Rev. 434 (1981)

Comment,
In re D.L.L. & C.L.L., Minors: Ruling on the
Constitutionality of the Indian Child Welfare Act.
26 S.D.L. Rev. 67 (1981)

Article XXVI
Schedule and Ordinance

Clinton,
State Power over Indian Reservations: A Critical
Comment on Burger Court Doctrine.
26 S.D.L. Rev. 434 (1981)

TENNESSEE

Chapter Forty-two
TENNESSEE CONSTITUTION- 1870

Article I
Declaration of Rights

Lewis,
Prichard v. Rogers and the Nightmare of Defective
Trust Deed Forms.
21 Tenn. B.J. 17 (1985)

Kritchevsky,
Justiciability in Tennessee, Part Two: Standing.
15 Mem. St. U.L. Rev. 179 (1985)

Kritchevsky,
Justiciability in Tennessee, Part One: Principles and
Limits.
15 Mem. St. U.L. Rev. 1 (1984)

Comment,
Confusing Views: Open View, Plain View, and Open
Fields Doctrines in Tennessee.
14 Mem. St. U.L. Rev. 337 (1984)

Comment,
Methods of Judicial Review Over Administrative
Actions in Tennessee.
13 Mem. St. U.L. Rev. 657 (1984)

Comment,
Government - Smith County Education Association
v. Anderson: An Exception Under the Tennessee
Open Meeting Act.
15 Mem. St. U.L. Rev. 116 (1984)

Comment,
Criminal Procedure - Search and
Seizure: The Good Faith Exception to the
Exclusionary Rule - How Should Tennessee Decide?
14 Mem. St. U.L. Rev. 549 (1984)

Currier,
"We Have a Warrant to Search Your Files!"
19 Tenn. B.J. 12 (1983)

King,
Constitutional law - Limitation of Actions-
Application of the Vested Rights Doctrine.
51 Tenn. L. Rev. 129 (1983)

Wurz,
Tennessee Criminal Constitutional Law from 1974-
1980: A Survey and Analysis.
12 Mem. St. U.L. Rev. 249 (1982)

Comment,
Satisfying the State Interest in Education with
Private Schools.
49 Tenn. L. Rev. 955 (1982)

Comment,
Tennessee Judicial Activism: Renaissance of
Federalism.
49 Tenn. L. Rev. 135 (1981)

Article II
Distribution of Powers

Kritchevsky,
Justiciability in Tennessee, Part Two: Standing.
15 Mem. St. U.L. Rev. 179 (1985)

Kritchevsky,
Government - Smith County Education Association
v. Anderson: An Exception Under the Tennessee
Open Meeting Act.
15 Mem. St. U.L. Rev. 179 (1984)

Kritchevsky,
Justiciability in Tennessee, Part One: Principles and
LImits.
15 Mem. St. U.L. Rev. 1 (1984)

Comment,
Methods of Judicial Review Over Administrative
Actions in Tennessee.
13 Mem. St. U.L. Rev. 657 (1984)

Feldman,
The Tennessee Pretrial Diversion Act: A
Practitioner's Guide.
13 Mem. St. U.L. Rev. 285 (1983)

Article III
Executive Department

Kritchevsky,
Justiciability in Tennessee, Part Two: Standing.
15 Mem. St. U.L. Rev. 179 (1985)

Beasley,
Remedies Other than the Tennessee Uniform
Administrative Procedures Act "Contested Case"
Approach to Dealing with State and Local
Governmental Action.
13 Mem. St. U.L. Rev. 619 (1984)

Article V
Impeachments

Kritchevsky,
Justiciability in Tennessee, Part One: Principles and
Limits.
15 Mem. St. U.L. Rev. 1 (1984)

Article VI
Judicial Department

Kritchevsky,
Justiciability in Tennessee, Part Two: Standing.
15 Mem. St. U.L. Rev. 179 (1985)

Bates,
Disqualification of Administrative Officers.
13 Mem. St. U.L. Rev. 501 (1984)

Beasley,
Remedies Other than the Tennessee Uniform
Administrative Procedures Act "Contested Case"
Approach to Dealing with State and Local
Governmental Action.
13 Mem. St. U.L. Rev. 619 (1984)

Article X
Oaths, Bribery of Electors, New Counties

Kritchevsky,
Justiciability in Tennessee, Part Two: Standing.
15 Mem. St. U.L. Rev. 179 (1985)

Article XI
Miscellaneous Provisions

Kritchevsky,
Justiciability in Tennessee, Part One: Principles and
Limits.
15 Mem. St. U.L. Rev. 1 (1984)

Ray,
Exempt Property in Tennessee Under the Bankruptcy
Code.
18 Tenn. B.J. 7 (1982)

Wurz,
Tennessee Criminal Constitutional Law from 1974-
1980: A Survey and Analysis.
12 Mem. St. U.L. Rev. 249 (1982)

Comment,
Satisfying the State Interest in Education with
Private Schools.
49 Tenn. L. Rev. 955 (1982)

TEXAS

Chapter Forty-three
TEXAS CONSTITUTION - 1876

Article I
Bill of Rights

Harrington,
The Texas Bill of Rights and Civil Liberties.
17 Tex. Tech L. Rev. 1487 (1986)

Comment,
Current Status of Open Courts Provision and
Discovery Rule.
16 Tex. Tech L. Rev. 765 (1985)

Harris,
Supreme Court's Search and Seizure Decisions of
1982 Term: Emergence of New Theory of Fourth
Amendment.
36 Baylor L. Rev. 41 (1984)

McColloch,
Annual Survey of Texas Law: Criminal Procedure.
38 Sw. L.J. (Tex.) 529 (1984)

Comment,
Is New Texas Drunk Driving Statute
Unconstitutional?
36 Baylor L. Rev. 565 (1984)

Butler,
Annual Survey of Texas Law: Real Property--
Condemnation and Restrictive Covenants.
37 Sw. L.J. (Tex.) 49 (1983)

Conley,
Annual Survey of Texas Law: Local Government
Law--Access to Government Information.
37 Sw. L.J. (Tex.) 325 (1983)

Dix,
Texas   Charging   Instrument   Law: Recent
Developments and Continuing Need for Reform.
35 Baylor L. Rev. 689 (1983)

Schoen,
Texas Equal Rights Amendment After First Decade:
Judicial Developments 1978-1982.
20 Hous. L. Rev. 1321 (1983)

Weston,
Vertical Distribution Restraints and Texas Antitrust
Laws.
37 Sw. L.J. (Tex.) 601 (1983)

Aycock,
Constitutionality of Requiring Park Dedication as
Condition of Plat Approval.
45 Tex. B.J. 721 (1982)

Bridge,
Annual Survey of Texas Law: Criminal Procedure.
36 Sw. L.J. (Tex.) 545 (1982)

Newman,
A Farewell To Arms? - Analysis of Texas Handgun
Control Law.
13 St. Mary's L.J. 601 (1982)

Comment,
Indictments and Motions to Quash: Problems of
Thomas v. State and Ferguson v. State.
34 Baylor L. Rev. 459 (1982)

Alexander,
Interlocutory Appellate Review of Double Jeopardy
Claims: Method for Testing Evidentiary Sufficiency
after Non-final Criminal Proceeding.
44 Tex. B.J. 11 (1981)

Babcock,
Annual Survey of Texas Law: Tort Liability.
35 Sw. L.J. (Tex.) 452 (1981)

Bubany,
Excluding Criminal Evidence: Can Private Searches
Poison the Fruit?
12 Tex. Tech L. Rev. 611 (1981)

Campbell and Edwards,
The Right to a Speedy Trial: An Overview of the
Texas Act.
44 Tex. B.J. 152 (1981)

Clinton,
Speedy Trial, Texas Style.
33 Baylor L. Rev. 707 (1981)

Collins,
Annual Survey of Texas Law: Local Government
Employees.
35 Sw. L.J. (Tex.) 440 (1981)

Collins,
Annual Survey of Texas Law: Workers'
Compensation.
35 Sw. L.J. (Tex.) 273 (1981)

Collins,
Right to Bail.
18 Hous. L. Rev. 495 (1981)

DeFoor,
Counsel, Dual Representation.
18 Hous. L. Rev. 519 (1981)

Denny,
Annual Survey of Texas Law: Liability Insurance.
35 Sw. L.J. (Tex.) 245 (1981)

McKnight,
Annual Survey of Texas Law: Divorce Proceedings.
35 Sw. L.J. (Tex.) 121 (1981)

Richards,
Equal Protection and Racial Quotas: Where Does
Fullilove v. Klutznick Leave Us?
33 Baylor L. Rev. 601 (1981)

Solender,
Annual Survey of Texas Law: Termination of
Parental Relationship and Adoption.
35 Sw. L.J. (Tex.) 171 (1981)

Steele,
Jeopardy Defense.
12 Tex. Tech L. Rev. 393 (1981)

Comment,
Indictment Process.
33 Baylor L. Rev. 1001 (1981)

Comment,
Required   Dedication   of   Park   Land: An
Unconstitutional Taking in Texas.
19 Hous. L. Rev. 175 (1981)

Baker,
Neutrality,   Process,   and   Rationality: Flawed
Interpretations of Equal Protection.
58 Tex. L. Rev. 1029 (1980)

McKnight,
Annual Survey of Texas Law: Family Law--Husband
and Wife.
34 Sw. L.J. (Tex.) 115 (1980)

Solender,
Annual Survey of Texas Law: Family Law--Parent
and Child.
34 Sw. L.J. (Tex.) 159 (1980)

Comment,
Defamation and Media Defendants in Texas.
34 Sw. L.J. (Tex.) 847 (1980)

Comment,
Regulating   Commercial   Speech: Conceptual
Framework for Analysis.
32 Baylor L. Rev. 235 (1980)

Comment,
Constitutional Limitations on Automobile Inventories.
21 S. Tex. L.J. 298 (1980)

Comment,
Property Division Obligations and the Constitutional
Prohibition on Imprisonment for Debt.
58 Tex. L. Rev. 1307 (1980)

Article II
The Powers of Government

Hill,
Annual Survey of Texas Law: Administrative Law.
34 Sw. L.J. (Tex.) 471 (1980)

Article III
Legislative Department

Babcock,
Annual Survey of Texas Law: Election Law.
35 Sw. L.J. (Tex.) 422 (1981)

Bickerstaff,
Reapportionment by State Legislatures: Guide for
the 1980's.
34 Sw. L.J. (Tex.) 607 (1980)

Article V
Judicial Department

Dix,
Appellate Review by Mandamus and Prohibition in
Texas Criminal Litigation.
17 Tex. Tech L. Rev. 75 (1986)

Robertson,
Discretionary Jurisdiction for the Texas Supreme
Court?
49 Tex. B.J. 210 (1986)

Gellis,
Reasons for Case Reversal in Texas: An Analysis.
16 St. Mary's L.J. 299 (1985)

McColloch,
Annual Survey of Texas Law: Criminal Procedure.
38 Sw. L.J. (Tex.) 529 (1984)

Hill,
Annual Survey of Texas Law: Administrative Law.
36 Sw. L.J. (Tex.) 527 (1982)

Campbell,
Right to Speedy Trial: Overview of Texas Act.
44 Tex. B.J. 152 (1981)

Dally,
Changes in Appellate Review in Criminal Cases
Following 1980 Constitutional Amendment.
13 St. Mary's L.J. 211 (1981)

Figari,
Annual Survey of Texas Law: Disqualification of
Trial Judge.
35 Sw. L.J. (Tex.) 381 (1981)

Galvin,
Annual Survey of Texas Law: Wills.
35 Sw. L.J. (Tex.) 21 (1981)

Huttash,
A Review of the Creation and Enactment of Post-
Trial and Appellate Statutes and Rules Applicable to
Criminal Cases.
33 Baylor L. Rev. 843 (1981)

McColl,
Criminal Post-trial and Appellate Procedure:
Practice Under New Texas Rules.
44 Tex. B.J. 1208 (1981)

McKnight,
Annual Survey of Texas Law: Divorce Proceedings.
35 Sw. L.J. (Tex.) 121 (1981)

Newton,
Annual Survey of Texas Law: Foreign Judgments.
35 Sw. L.J. (Tex.) 353 (1981)

Sparks,
Judicial Refusal: Rule 18a--Substance or Procedure.
12 St. Mary's L.J. 723 (1981)

Comment,
Indictment Process.
33 Baylor L. Rev. 1001 (1981)

Calvert,
Jurisdiction of the Texas Supreme Court in Divorce
Cases.
33 Baylor L. Rev. 51 (1980)

Figari,
Annual Survey of Texas Law: Civil Procedure.
34 Sw. L.J. (Tex.) 415 (1980)

Schwab,
Who Determines Judicial Disqualification?
43 Tex. B.J. 197 (1980)

Soules,
Rule 18a: Recusal or Disqualification of Trial Judge.
43 Tex. B.J. 1005 (1980)

Comment,
Declaratory Judgments from the Texas Court of
Criminal Appeals.
21 S. Tex. L.J. 310 (1980)

Article VIII
Taxation and Revenue

Popp,
Determination of Situs, Jurisdiction and Allocation
for Ad Valorem Taxation of Personal Property.
46 Tex. B.J. 1260 (1983)

McKnight,
Annual Survey of Texas Law: Family Law--Husband
and Wife.
36 Sw. L.J. (Tex.) 97 (1982)

Stark,
Annual Survey of Texas Law: Taxation.
36 Sw. L.J. (Tex.) 571 (1982)

Saunders,
1981 Legislation: Real Property.
44 Tex. B.J. 1203 (1981)

Article XI
Municipal Corporations

Ashcroft,
Home Rule Cities and Municipal Annexation in
Texas: Recent Trends and Future Prospects.
15 St. Mary's L.J. 519 (1984)

Babcock,
Annual Survey of Texas Law: Election Law.
35 Sw. L.J. (Tex.) 422 (1981)

Article XII
Private Corporations

Folladori,
Annual Survey of Texas Law: Corporations and
Partnerships.
35 Sw. L.J. (Tex.) 225 (1981)

Article XVI
General Provisions

Soronen,
Amendment to Article XVI of the Texas
Constitution: Greater Uniformity Among the
Community Property States.
21 S. Tex. L.J. 239 (1981)

Article XVII
Mode of Amending the Constitution of this State

Vaughan,
Texas Amends Its Constitution and Its Community
Property System.
8 Comm. Property J. 59 (1981)

UTAH

Chapter Forty-four

UTAH CONSTITUTION - 1895

Article I
Declaration of Rights

Comment,
Confrontation Rights and Preliminary Hearings.
1986 Utah L. Rev. 75 (1986)

Comment,
The Individual Right to Bear Arms: An Illusory
Public Pacifier?
1986 Utah L. Rev. 751 (1986)

Comment,
The Utah Supreme Court and the Utah State
Constitution.
1986 Utah L. Rev. 739 (1986)

Comment,
Recent Developments in Utah Law.
1986 Utah L. Rev., 199 (1986)

Comment,
KUTV v. Wilkinson: Another Episode in the Fair
Trial/Free Press Saga.
1985 Utah L. Rev. 739 (1985)

Comment,
Judicial Jabberwocky or Uniform Constitutional
Protection?   Strickland v. Washington and National
Standards for Ineffective Assistance of Counsel
Claims.
1985 Utah L. Rev. 723 (1985)

Crabb,
Religious Symbols, American Traditions and the
Constitution.
1984 B.Y.U. L. Rev. 509 (1984)

Swift,
Restraints on Defense Publicity in Criminal Jury
Cases.
1984 Utah L. Rev. 45 (1984)

Graham,
Restatement of the Intended Meaning of the
Establishment Clause in Relation to Education and
Religion.
1981 B.Y.U. L. Rev. 333 (1981)

Oaks,
Trust Doctrines in Church Controversies.
1981 B.Y.U. L. Rev. 805 (1981)

Comment,
Revocation of Tax-Exempt Status of Religious
Schools - Conflict with the Religion Clauses of the
First Amendment: Bob Jones University v. United
States.
1981 B.Y.U. L. Rev. 949 (1981)

Comment,
Hansen   v.   Owens--Expansion   of   the   Privilege
Against Self-Incrimination to Unknown Limits.
1981 Utah L. Rev. 447 (1981)

Comment,
The Impact of Expanded Rules for Determining what
Constitutes the "Same Offense" for Double Jeopardy
Purposes: Illinois v. Vitale.
1980 B.Y.U. L. Rev. 948 (1980)

Marsden,
The   Utah   Supreme   Court   and   the   Utah   State
Constitution.
1986 Utah L. Rev. 319 (1986)

Article X
Education

Graham,
Restatement of the Intended Meaning of the
Establishment Clause in Relation to Education and
Religion.
1981 B.Y.U. L. Rev. 333 (1981)

Comment,
Revocation of Tax-Exempt Status of Religious
Schools - Conflict with the Religion Clauses of the
First Amendment: Bob Jones University v. United
States.
1981 B.Y.U. L. Rev. 949 (1981)

Article XI
Counties, Cities and Towns

Comment,
CP National Corp. v. Public Service Commission:
The Jurisdictional Ambiguity Surrounding Municipal
Power Systems.
1982 Utah L. Rev. 913 (1982)

Comment,
State v. Hutchinson - Redefining the Scope of Local
Regulatory Power.
1981 Utah L. Rev. 617 (1981)

Article XX
Public Lands

McCormack,
Land Use Planning and Management of State School
Lands.
1982 Utah L. Rev. 525 (1982)

VERMONT

Chapter Forty-five
VERMONT CONSTITUTION - 1793

Chapter I.
A Declaration of the Rights of the Inhabitants
of the State of Vermont

Comment,
Victimizing the Child Victim: Vermont Rule of
Evidence 807 and Trauma in the Courtroom.
11 Vt. L. Rev. 631 (1986)

Comment,
Victims' Rights: Vermont's New Law.
11 Vt. L. Rev. 695 (1986)

Comment,
The Proposed Administrative License Suspension
Procedures in Vermont: How Much Process are
Drunken Drivers Due?
11 Vt. L. Rev. 75 (1986)

Halbrook,
The Right to Bear Arms in the First State Bills of
Rights: Pennsylvania, North Carolina, Vermont, and
Massachusetts.
10 Vt. L. Rev. 255 (1985)

Comment,
Grandparents'   Statutory   Right   to   Petition   for
Visitation: Vermont and the National Framework.
10 Vt. L. Rev. 55 (1985)

Comment,
Medical   Malpractice,   Contract   or   Tort: The
Vermont Statute of Frauds.
10 Vt. L. Rev. 99 (1985)

Comment,
Toxic Substance Safety Statute Violations: Should
Vermont Adopt the Negligence Per Se With Excuse
Doctrine?
10 Vt. L. Rev. 151 (1985)

Comment,
Protecting Liberty Interests: Developments in
Vermont's Mental Health Law as Federal
Constitutional Protection Declines.
9 Vt. L. Rev. 265 (1984)

Comment,
Post-Traumatic Stress Disorder as an Insanity
Defense in Vermont.
9 Vt. L. Rev. 69 (1984)

Comment,
The Serious Young Offender Under Vermont's
Juvenile Law: Beyond the Reach of Parens Patriae.
8 Vt. L. Rev. 173 (1983)

Comment,
Recreational Rights In Public Water Overlying
Private Property.
8 Vt. L. Rev. 301 (1983)

Comment,
Restricting the Right to Bail: Vermont's New
Constitutional Bail Amendment.
8 Vt. L. Rev. 347 (1983)

Comment,
Due Process and Vermont's Abuse Prevention
Statute.
7 Vt. L. Rev. 185 (1982)

Comment,
Abortion Choice and the Law in Vermont: A
Recent Study.
7 Vt. L. Rev. 281 (1982)

Kreiling,
State v. Whitingham School Board: A Unique
Employment Discrimination Loophole for Vermont
Employers.
6 Vt. L. Rev. 119 (1981)

Comment,
The Standard of Review in Equal Protection and
Due Process Challenges to Vermont's Blue Laws.
6 Vt. L. Rev. 173 (1981)

Comment,
Do Sixteen and Seventeen Year Old Criminal
Defendants in Vermont Need a Guardian Ad Litem?
5 Vt. L. Rev. 361 (1980)

Chapter II.
Plan or Frame of Government:
Legislative Department

Comment,
Legislative Review of Agency Rule-Making:
Vermont's Antlerless Deer Hunting Regulation.
11 Vt. L. Rev. 105 (1986)

Comment,
A Critique of the Vermont Securities Act: Is
Vermont's Blue Sky Really Grey?
11 Vt. L. Rev. 131 (1986)

Dooley,
The Regulation of the Practice of Law, Practice and
Procedure, and Court Administration in Vermont--
Judicial or Legislative Power?
8 Vt. L. Rev. 211 (1983)

Comment,
State Regulation of Private Church Schools: An
Examination of Vermont's Act 151.
8 Vt. L. Rev. 75 (1983)

Comment,
The Need for Exacting Legislation Regulating the
Shipment of Radioactive Wastes in Vermont.
8 Vt. L. Rev. 407 (1983)

Comment,
Legislative Control Over the Uranium Industry in
Vermont: Flirting with Preemption.
7 Vt. L. Rev. 315 (1982)

Comment,
No Contribution Among Joint Tortfeasors: The Fule
that has Fooled the Courts and Foiled the Vermont
Legislature.
7 Vt. L. Rev. 337 (1982)

Comment,
Regulation of Energy Developments in the Green
Mountain national Forest: Is Vermont Law
Preempted?
7 Vt. L. Rev. 97 (1982)

Comment,
Vagueness and Overbreadth: The Constitutional
Challenges to Vermont's Land Use and Development
Law(Act 250).
5 Vt. L. Rev. 329 (1980)

Chapter II.
Plan or Frame of Government:
Judiciary Department

Comment,
The Vermont Supreme Court: "Guilty" of Judicial
legislating?
11 Vt. L. Rev. 661 (1986)

Norten,
An Automated Standing Rule May be Promulgated
Under Article 11 of the Vermont Constitution.
10 Vt. L. Rev. 459 (1985)

Soltan,
Precedent and the Jewett Admonition.
10 Vt. L. Rev. 447 (1985)

Comment,
Jurisdiction Over Adjudications Involving the
Abenaki Indians of Vermont.
10 Vt. L. Rev. 417 (1985)

Smith and Connolly,
Caseflow Management and Backlog Reduction: An
Examination of Vermont's Superior Court program.
9 Vt. L. Rev. 247 (1984)

Dooley,
The Regulation of the Practice of Law, Practice and
Procedure, and Court Administration in Vermont--
Judicial or Legislative Power?
8 Vt. L. Rev. 211 (1983)

Comment,
Vermont's Children in Need of Care or Supervision:
Judicial Discretion or Definition?
8 Vt. L. Rev. 119 (1983)

Comment,
Judicial Review of Criminal Convictions Based on
Circumstantial Evidence.
6 Vt. L. Rev. 197 (1981)

VIRGINIA

Chapter Forty-six
VIRGINIA CONSTITUTION - 1970

Article I
Bill of Rights

Pagan,
Civil Rights and "Personal Injuries": Virginia's
Statute of LImitations for Section 1983 Suits.
26 Wm. & Mary L. Rev. 199 (1985)

Schnapper,
Unreasonable Search and Seizures of Papers.
71 Va. L. Rev. 869 (1985)

Comment,
The Myth of Religious Neutrality by Separation in
Education.
71 Va. L. Rev. 127 (1985)

Comment,
Enforcing Separation of Church and State Through
State Constitutional Provisions.
71 Va. L. Rev. 625 (1985)

Comment,
The New Doctrine of Necessaries in Virginia.
19 U. Rich. L. Rev. 317 (1985)

McFarlane,
Benign Racial Classifications: A Guide for
Transportation Attorneys.
19 U. Rich L. Rev. 29 (1984)

Livingston,
Public Access to Virginia's Tidelands.
24 Wm. & Mary L. Rev. 669 (1983)

Williams,
State Constitutional Law Processes.
24 Wm. & Mary L. Rev. 169 (1983)

Comment,
Eminent Domain and Water Allocation as Related to
Coal Slurry Pipelines.
17 U. Rich. L. Rev. 789 (1983)

Comment,
Immediate Appeal from Counsel Disqualification in
Criminal Cases.
25 Wm. & Mary L. Rev. 131 (1983)

Comment,
Separation   of   Powers   Aspects   of   Service   by
Legislators on Administrative Boards.
40 Wash. & Lee L. Rev. 171 (1983)

Johnson,
Virginia Laws Affecting Churches.
17 U. Rich. L. Rev. 1 (1982)

Comment,
Stop and Frisk Based Upon Anonymous Telephone
Tips.
39 Wash. & Lee L. Rev. 1437 (1982)

Comment,
Prejudicial Effects of Cameras in the Courtroom.
16 U. Rich. L. Rev. 867 (1982)

Comment,
Double Jeopardy and the Virginia Supreme Court's
Approaches to Multiple Punishment.
16 U. Rich. L. Rev. 885 (1982)

Bryson,
Discovery Penalties.
15 U. Rich. L. Rev. 283 (1981)

Halbrook,
Jurisprudence   of   the   Second   and   Fourteenth
Amendments.
4 Geo. Mason L. Rev. 1 (1981)

Taylor,
Re-examination   of   Sovereign   Tort   Immunity   in
Virginia.
15 U. Rich. L. Rev. 247 (1981)

Comment,
Criminal Procedure and Criminal Law: Virginia
Supreme Court Decisions During the 70's.
15 U. Rich. L. Rev. 585 (1981)

Comment,
Public Access to Criminal Trials.
15 U. Rich. L. Rev. 741 (1981)

Comment,
Overview of Virginia Supreme Court Decisions on
Domestic Relations.
15 U. Rich. L. Rev. 423 (1981)

Comment,
Constitutional Analysis of Virginia's Medical
Malpractice Act.
37 Wash. & Lee L. Rev. 1192 (1980)

Article II
Franchise and Officers

Comment,
Enforcing Separation of Church and State Through
State Constitutional Provisions.
71 Va. L. Rev. 625 (1985)

O'Rourke,
Voting Rights Act Amendments of 1982: The New
Bailout Provision and Virginia.
69 Va. L. Rev. 765 (1983)

Levinson,
Legislative and Executive Veto of Rules of
Administrative Agencies: Models and Alternatives.
24 Wm. & Mary L. Rev. 79 (1982)

Parker,
The Virginia Legislative Reapportionment Case:
Reapportionment Issues of the 1980's.
5 Geo. Mason L. Rev. 1 (1982)

Comment,
1981 Redistricting Process in Virginia.
68 Va. L. Rev. 541 (1982)

Article V
Executive

Williams,
State Constitutional Law Processes.
24 Wm. & Mary L. Rev. 169 (1983)

Levinson,
Legislative and Executive Veto of Rules of Administrative Agencies:1979.
66 Va. L. Rev. 367 (1980)

Article VI
Judiciary

Pagan,
Civil rights and personal Injuries: Virginia's Stature of Limitations for Section 1983 suits.
28 Wm. & Mary L. Rev. 199 (1985)

Williams,
State Constitutional Law Process.
24 Wm. & Mary L. Rev. 169 (1983)

Comment,
Prohibition: The elusive and Misunderstood Writ.
16 U. Rich. L. Rev. 693 (1982)

Comment,
Virginia Judicial Council's Intermediate Appellate Court Proposal.
16 U. Rich L. Rev. 209 (1982)

Article VII
Local Government

Williams,
State Constitutional Law Processes.
24 Wm. & Mary L. REv. 169 (1983)

Brown,
Constitutional Zoning in Virginia.
16 U. Rich. L. Rev. 117 (1982)

Butler,
Common-Law Principles Underlying Public Interest in Tidal Water Resources.
23 Wm. & Mary L. Rev. 835 (1982)

Comment,
Need for Reform in Virginia of Rule Which Limits the Power of Municipal Governments to Express Grants of Statutory Authority.
68 Va. L. Rev. 693 (1982)

Article VIII
Education

Comment,
Enforcing Separation of church and State Through State Constitutional Provisions.
71 Va. L. Rev. 625 (1985)

Williams,
State Constitutional Law Processes.
24 Wm. & Mary L. Rev. 169 (1983)

Comment,
Working to the Contract in Virginia: Legal Consequences of Teachers Attempts to LImit Their Contractual Duties.
16 U. Rich. L. Rev. 449 (1982)

Article IX
Corporations

Comment,
Survey of Virginia Administrative Law and Utility Regulation for the Year 1978-1979.
66 Va. L. Rev. 193 (1980)

Article X
Taxation and Finance

Johnson,
Virginia Tax Laws Affecting Churches.
18 U. Rich. L. Rev. 301 (1984)

Williams,
State Constitutional Law Processes.
24 Wm. & Mary L. Rev. 169 (1983)

Comment,
Survey of Virginia Law on Taxation for the year
1978-1979.
66 Va. L. Rev. 367 (1980)

Article XI
Conservation

Livingston,
Public Access to Virginia's Tidelands.
24 Wm. & Mary L. Rev. 669 (1983)

Comment,
Eminent Domain and Water Allocation as Related to
Coal Slurry Pipelines.
17 U. Rich. L. Rev. 789 (1983)

Butler,
Common-Law Principles Underlying Public Interest
in Tidal Water Resources.
23 Wm. & Mary L. Rev. 835 (1982)

McGovern,
Issues Relating to Toxic Substances Litigation,
Focusing on the Fourth Circuit.
16 U. Rich. L. Rev. 247 (1982)

Article XII
Future Changes

Williams,
State Constitutional Law Processes.
24 Wm. & Mary L. Rev. 169 (1983)

WASHINGTON

Chapter Forty-seven
WASHINGTON CONSTITUTION - 1889

Article I
Declaration of Rights

Dolliver,
The Washington Constitution and "State Action":
The View of the Gramers.
22 Willamette L. Rev. 445 (1986)

Nock,
Seizing Opportunity, Searching for Theory: Article
I, Section 7.
8 Puget Sound L. Rev. 331 (1985)

Proebsting,
Washington's Equal Rights Amendment: It Says
What It Means and It Means What it Says.
8 Puget Sound L. Rev. 461 (1985)

Utter,
Independent   Interpretation   of   the   Washington
Declaration of Rights.
7 Puget Sound L. Rev. 491 (1984)

Comment,
Protective Orders: Media Publication of Discovered
Information.
8 Puget Sound L. Rev. 123 (1984)

Comment,
Scope   of   Commerce   Clause   in   International
Commerce.
55 Wash. L. Rev. 885 (1984)

Comment,
New Limits on Police Vehicle Searches.
60 Wash. L. Rev. 177 (1984)

Engdahl,
Foundations for Military Intervention in the United
States.
7 Puget Sound L. Rev. 1 (1983)

Sax,
Decline of Private Property.
58 Wash. L. Rev. 481 (1983)

Comment,
Washington Recognizes Wrongful Birth and Wrongful
Life: A Critical Analysis.
58 Wash. L. Rev. 649 (1983)

Comment,
Refusal to Accept Advertising: Restraint of Trade
Versus Free Press.
7 Puget Sound L. Rev. 211 (1983)

Comment,
Free Speech, Initiative and Property Rights in
Conflict.
58 Wash. L. Rev. 587 (1983)

Comment,
New Life for the Doctrine of Unconstitutional
Conditions?
58 Wash. L. Rev. 679 (1983)

Comment,
Dimensions of a Journalist's Shield.
6 Puget Sound L. Rev. 285 (1983)

Adams,
Search and Seizure.
6 Puget Sound L. Rev. 1 (1982)

Buchanan,
What Constitutes State Action?
57 Wash. L. Rev. 245 (1982)

Burke,
Criminal Law: Warrantless Detention.
17 Gonz. L. Rev. 555 (1982)

Cohen,
Cameras in the Courtroom.
57 Wash. L. Rev. 277 (1982)

Kirst,
Jury's Historic Domain in Complex Cases.
58 Wash. L. Rev. 1 (1982)

Kuger,
Constitutional Law: Sex Discrimination.
17 Gonz. L. Rev. 763 (1982)

Morris,
Exclusionary Rule: Assessment of Social Cost.
57 Wash. L. Rev. 647 (1982)

Posner,
Excessive Sanctions for Governmental Misconduct in Criminal Cases.
57 Wash. L. Rev. 635 (1982)

Youngmun,
Criminal Law: Merger of Crimes.
17 Gonz. L. Rev. 547 (1982)

Comment,
Washington Conditions Media Access to the Courtroom.
57 Wash. L. Rev. 759 (1982)

Comment,
News-Source Privilege in Libel Cases.
57 Wash. L. Rev. 349 (1982)

Comment,
Is Inverse Condemnation An Appropriate Remedy for Due Process Violations?
57 Wash. L. Rev. 551 (1982)

Comment,
Recidivist Statutes: Application of Proportionality and Overbreadth Doctrines.
57 Wash. L. Rev. 573 (1982)

Comment,
Balancing Right to Interrogate Against the Right to Counsel.
17 Gonz. L. Rev. 697 (1982)

Comment,
Testing the Constitutionality of Land Use
Regulations.
57 Wash. L. Rev. 715 (1982)

Boe,
Criminal Law: Collateral Estoppel.
16 Gonz. L. Rev. 757 (1981)

Collings,
Criminal Law: Roadblocks: Automobile Search and
Seizure.
16 Gonz. L. Rev. 437 (1981)

Cullitan,
Evidence: Recording Private Conversations.
16 Gonz. L. Rev. 797 (1981)

Erickson,
Criminal Law: Search and Seizure.
16 Gonz. L. Rev. 785 (1981)

Galdasty,
The Deceptive Right to Know: How Pessimism
Rewrote the First Amendment.
56 Wash. L. Rev. 365 (1981)

Harris,
Washington's Doctrine of Corporate Disregard.
54 Wash. L. Rev. 253 (1981)

Lollis,
Constitutional Law: Juvenile Waiver of Rights.
16 Gonz. L. Rev. 415 (1981)

Riga,
Capital Punishment and the Right to Life as
Absolute.
5 Puget Sound L. Rev. 23 (1981)

Comment,
Electronic Fund Transfers and the Right to
Financial Privacy.
16 Gonz. L. Rev. 313 (1981)

Comment,
Washington's New DWI Statute: Does Due Process
Mandate Preservation of Breathalyzer Ampoules?
16 Gonz. L. Rev. 357 (1981)

Comment,
Void-For-Vagueness Issue: Judicial Response To
Allegedly Vague Statutes.
56 Wash. L. Rev. 131 (1980-81)

Comment,
Defamation and the First Amendment: Protecting
Speech on Public Issues Versus Defamation.
56 Wash. L. Rev. 75 (1980-81)

Baum,
Criminal Law: Pro Se Representation.
15 Gonz. L. Rev. 565 (1980)

Boyer,
Criminal Law - Motor Vehicles.
16 Gonz. L. Rev. 227 (1980)

Coggins,
Federal Wildlife Law and the Constitution.
55 Wash. L. Rev. 295 (1980)

Hugg,
Thinking Clearly about Privacy.
55 Wash. L. Rev. 777 (1980)

Rohall,
Carriers: Search and Seizure.
15 Gonz. L. Rev. 881 (1980)

Woodard,
Knock and Announce in Washington.
15 Gonz. L. Rev. 1041 (1980)

Comment,
The Broadening of the Pentagon Papers Standard:
An Impermissible Misapplication of the National
Security Exception to the Prior Restraint Doctrine.
4 Puget Sound L. Rev. 123 (1980)

Comment,
Search and Seizure: Good   Faith   of   Officer   as
Affecting Admissibility.
55 Wash. L. Rev. 849 (1980)

Comment,
Criminal Procedure - Luggage Found During a
Lawful Warrantless Search of An Automobile May
Not Be Searched Without a Warrant.
55 Wash. L. Rev. 871 (1980)

Article II
Legislative Department

Comment,
Jurisdiction of State Courts over Other States.
56 Wash. L. Rev. 289 (1981)

Williams,
Emotional   Distress   Resulting   from   Disciplinary
Actions by Officers of State Militia: Liability of
State.
15 Gonz. L. Rev. 947 (1980)

Article IV
The Judiciary

Comment,
Stare   Decisis   in   Lower   Courts: Predicting   the
Demise of Supreme Court Precedent.
60 Wash. L. Rev. 87 (1984)

Horgan,
Remaking Reality in Prison Decisions.
17 Gonz. L. Rev. 639 (1982)

Spitzer,
Court Rulemaking.
6 Puget Sound L. Rev. 31 (1982)

Lamberson,
Jurisdiction: Sterilization of Mental Incompetents.
16 Gonz. L. Rev. 465 (1981)

Comment,
Ethical   Conduct   in   Judicial   Campaign: Is
Campaigning an Ethical Activity.
57 Wash. L. Rev. 119 (1981)

Comment,
Deciding   the   Retroactive   Effect   of   Overruling
Decisions.
55 Wash. L. Rev. 833 (1980)

Article VIII
State, County and Municipal Indebtedness

Spitzer,
An Analytical View of Recent "Lending of Credit"
Decisions in Washington State.
8 Puget Sound L. Rev. 195 (1985)

Reich,
Lending of Credit Reinterpreted: New Opportunities
for Public and Private Sector Cooperation.
19 Gonz. L. Rev. 639 (1983/84)

Article IX
Education

Comment,
Building Codes and Zoning Ordinances Applied to
Parochial Schools.
7 Puget Sound L. Rev. 607 (1984)

Comment,
Attack   on   the   Education   for   All   Handicapped
Children Act.
7 Puget Sound L. Rev. 183 (1983)

Comment,
Aid to Private Education.
16 Gonz. L. Rev. 171 (1980)

Article XI
County, City, and Township Organization

Comment,
Retaliatory Evictions in Washington and Seattle.
57 Wash. L. Rev. 293 (1982)

Keer,
Obscenity: State Preemption.
15 Gonz. L. Rev. 913 (1980)

Article XII
Corporations Other than Municipal

Reich,
Lending of Credit Reinterpreted: New Opportunities
for Public and Private Sector Cooperation.
19 Gonz. L. Rev. 639 (1983/84)

Erxleben,
Residential Real Estate Brokerage: Breaking   the
Cartel.
56 Wash. L. Rev. 179 (1981)

Wirtz,
Purpose and Effect in Sherman Act Conspiracies.
56 Wash. L. Rev. 1 (1981)

Article XVII
Tide Lands

Conklin,
Floating Down the River: In Re the Little Spokane.
17 Gonz. L. Rev. 869 (1982)

Article XXI
Water and Water Rights

Comment,
Towards a Unified Reasonable Use Approach to
Water Drainage in Washington.
59 Wash. L. Rev. 61 (1984)

Comment,
Protecting the People's Waters.
59 Wash. L. Rev. 357 (1984)

Conklin,
Floating Down the River: In Re The Little
Spokane.
17 Gonz. L. Rev. 869 (1982)

Comment,
Water Rights on Indian Reservations-
Transferability.
58 Wash. L. Rev. 89 (1982)

Trelease,
State Water laws Versus National Water Uses.
55 Wash. L. Rev. 751 (1980)

Article XXV
Jurisdiction

Trelease,
State Water Laws Versus National Water Uses.
55 Wash. L. Rev. 751 (1980)

Article XXVI
Compact with the United States

Comment,
Building Codes and Zoning Ordinances Applied to
Parochial Schools.
7 Puget Sound L. Rev. 607 (1984)

Sanders,
Northwest Power Act and Reserved Tribal Rights.
58 Wash. L. Rev. 357 (1983)

Barsh,
Cohen's Handbook of Federal Indian law: Book
Review.
57 Wash. L. Rev. 799 (1982)

Comment,
Water Rights on Indian Reservations-
Transferability.
58 Wash. L. Rev. 89 (1982)

Barsh,
Contrary   Jurisprudence: Tribal   Interests   in
Navigable   Waterways   Before   and   After   Montana   v.
United States.
56 Wash. L. Rev. 627 (1981)

Comment,
Pacific Northwest Indian Treaty Fishing Rights.
5 Puget Sound L. Rev. 99 (1981)

Trelease,
State Water Laws Versus National Water Uses.
55 Wash. L. Rev. 751 (1980)

Article XXXI
Sex Equality-Rights and Responsibilities

Chun,
Constitutional Law: Sex Discrimination.
15 Gonz. L. Rev. 1093 (1980)

WEST VIRGINIA

Chapter Forty-eight
WEST VIRGINIA CONSTITUTION - 1872

Article III
Bill of Rights

Esbeck,
Tort Claims Against Churches and Ecclesiastical
Officers: The First Amendment Considerations.
89 W. Va. L. Rev. 1 (1986)

Reid,
Law, Politics and the Homeless.
89 W. Va. L. Rev. 115 (1986)

McQueen,
Survey of Developments in West Virginia Law:
1985.
88 W. Va. L. Rev. 348 (1985)

Parker,
Survey of Developments in West Virginia Law:
1984.
87 W. Va. L. Rev. 506 (1985)

Perrone,
West Virginia's New Summary Eviction Proceedings:
New Questions For an Old Answer.
87 W. Va. L. Rev. 359 (1985)

Comment,
Ballot Access Laws in West Virginia - A Call for
Change.
87 W. Va. L. Rev. 809 (1985)

Artimez,
Developments in Criminal Procedure.
86 W. Va. L. Rev. 479 (1983)

Cokeley,
Developments in Tort Law.
86 W. Va. L. Rev. 479 (1983)

Crittenden,
Survey of Recent Developments in West Virginia
Law: Unreasonable Search and Seizure.
86 W. Va. L. Rev. 495 (1983)

Kinnaman,
Pauley v. Bailey: Towards a "Thorough and
Efficient" School System.
85 W. Va. L. Rev. 339 (1983)

McGowan,
Survey of Recent Development in West Virginia Law:
Miscellaneous (Criminal).
85 W. Va. L. Rev. 497 (1983)

Morris,
Survey of Recent Developments in West Virginia
Law: Presence.
85 W. Va. L. Rev. 496 (1983)

Morton,
Developments in Jury Law.
86 W. Va. L. Rev. 479 (1983)

Stoneking,
Developments in Employment Law.
86 W. Va. L. Rev. 479 (1983)

Williams,
Developments in Juvenile Law.
86 W. Va. L. Rev. 479 (1983)

Woodburn,
Survey of Recent Developments in West Virginia
Law: Due Process in Dismissals.
85 W. Va. L. Rev. 438 (1983)

Comment,
West v. National Mines: Creation of Private
Nuisance By Use of Public Property.
85 W. Va. L. Rev. 263 (1983)

Donahoe,
Speedy Trial.
84 W. Va. L. Rev. 551 (1982)

Farrell,
<u>Communication in the Courtroom: Jury Instructions</u>.
85 W. Va. L. Rev. 5 (1982)

Flannery and Poland,
<u>Hazardous Waste Management Act - Closing the
Circle</u>.
84 W. Va. L. Rev. 347 (1982)

Frame,
<u>Double Jeopardy and the Same Transaction Test</u>.
84 W. Va. L. Rev. 443 (1982)

Harrell,
<u>The Scrambling of Constitutional and Common Law
Defamation Analysis</u>.
84 W. Va. L. Rev. 849 (1982)

Clark,
<u>Elections</u>.
83 W. Va. L. Rev. 331 (1980)

Collias,
<u>Double Jeopardy in West Virginia: State Ex Rel.
Dowdy v. Robinson</u>.
83 W. Va. L. Rev. 259 (1980)

Fluharty,
<u>Domestic Relations</u>.
83 W. Va. L. Rev. 324 (1980)

Grill,
<u>Due Process Protection for Nontenured Faculty in
Public Institutions of Higher Education: Long
Overdue</u>.
83 W. Va. L. Rev. 99 (1980)

Harrell,
<u>The Public, the Media and the Criminal Defendant:
Access to Courtrooms Prevails Over Fears of
Prejudicial Publicity</u>.
83 W. Va. L. Rev. 245 (1980)

Traina,
<u>Constitutional Law</u>.
83 W. Va. L. Rev. 283 (1980)

Williams,
Administrative Law.
83 W. Va. L. Rev. 271 (1980)

Article V
Division of Powers

Perrone,
West Virginia's New Summary Eviction Proceedings:
New Questions for an Old Answer.
87 W. Va. L. Rev. 359 (1985)

Cokeley,
Developments in Statutory Construction.
86 W. Va. L. Rev. 479 (1983)

Stewart,
Survey of Recent Developments in West Virginia
Law: Public Service Commission Procedure.
85 W. Va. L. Rev. 412 (1983)

Ramey,
Constitutional Law.
84 W. Va. L. Rev. 560 (1982)

Article VI
The Legislature

Lorenson,
Survey of Developments in West Virginia Law:
1984.
87 W. Va. L. Rev. 550 (1985)

Comment,
Tort Liability of Institutional Review Boards.
87 W. Va. L. Rev. 137 (1984)

Artimez,
Developments in Commercial Law.
86 W. Va. L. Rev. 479 (1983)

Stewart,
Survey of Recent Developments in West Virginia
Law: School Board Immunity.
85 W. Va. L. Rev. 417 (1983)

Comment,
Teachers' Union and Employment Rights: A Survey
of West Virginia Law.
85 W. Va. L. Rev. 239 (1983)

Comment,
West v. National Mines: Creation of Private
Nuisance By Use of Public Property.
85 W. Va. L. Rev. 263 (1983)

Flannery and Poland,
Hazardous Waste Management Act - Closing the
Circle.
84 W. Va. L. Rev. 347 (1982)

Bowman,
A Judicial Dilemma: Real or Imagined?
83 W. Va. L. Rev. 29 (1980)

Article VIII
Judicial Power

Hagan,
Policy Activism in the West Virginia Supreme Court
of Appeals, 1930-1985.
89 W. Va. L. Rev. 149 (1986)

Venezia,
Survey of Developments in West Virginia Law:
1985.
88 W. Va. L. Rev. 396 (1985)

Cokeley,
Developments in Statutory Construction.
86 W. Va. L. Rev. 479 (1983)

Frame,
Double Jeopardy and the Same Transaction Test.
84 W. Va. L. Rev. 443 (1982)

Starcher,
Cameras in the Courts.
84 W. Va. L. Rev. 267 (1982)

Bowman,
A Judicial Dilemma: Real or Imagined?
83 W. Va. L. Rev. 29 (1980)

Article X
Taxation and Finance

Hellems,
Survey of Developments in West Virginia Law:
1985.
88 W. Va. L. Rev. 457 (1985)

Moran,
Is Everyone Paying Their Fair Share?   An Analysis
of Taxpayers' Actions to Equalize Taxes.
85 W. Va. L. Rev. 209 (1983)

Turner,
Developments in Tax Law.
86 W. Va. L. Rev. 479 (1983)

Michael,
Agricultural Land Preservation by Local Government.
84 W. Va. L. Rev. 961 (1982)

Dorsey,
Taxation.
83 W. Va. L. Rev. 595 (1981)

Wakefield,
Problems Associated With the Management of Solid
Wastes: Is There a Solution in the Offing?
83 W. Va. L. Rev. 131 (1980)

White,
Revenue Bonds for Commercial Development in West
Virginia: The Endorsement by the West Virginia
Supreme Court of Appeals.
83 W. Va. L. Rev. 67 (1980)

Article XII
Education

Kinnaman,
Pauley v. Bailey: Towards a "Thorough and
Efficient" School System.
85 W. Va. L. Rev. 339 (1983)

Rothstein,
Right to Education for the Handicapped in West
Virginia.
85 W. Va. L. Rev. 187 (1983)

Flannery and Poland,
Hazardous Waste Management Act - Closing the
Circle.
84 W. Va. L. Rev. 347 (1982)

Ramey,
Constitutional Law.
84 W. Va. L. Rev. 560 (1982)

Article XIV
How Amendments Are Made

Comment,
Tort Liability of Institutional Review Boards.
87 W. Va. L. Rev. 137 (1984)

WISCONSIN

Chapter Forty-nine
WISCONSIN CONSTITUTION - 1848

Preamble

Comment,
Rediscovering   the   Wisconsin   Constitution:
Representation of Constitutional Questions in State
Courts.
1983 Wis. L. Rev. 483 (1983)

Article I
Declaration of Rights

Comment,
Corroborating Confessions: An Empirical Analysis
of Legal Safeguards Against False Confessions.
1984 Wis. L. Rev. 1121 (1984)

Comment,
Solem   v.   Helm: Supreme   Court   Extends
Proportionality   Requirement   to   Sentences   of
Imprisonment.
1984 Wis. L. Rev. 1401 (1984)

Comment,
Municipal Liability: Failure to Provide Adequate
Police Protection--Special Duty Doctrine Should be
Discarded.
1984 Wis. L. Rev. 499 (1984)

Comment,
Analyzing the Reasonableness of Bodily Intrusions.
68 Marq. L. Rev. 130 (1984)

Comment,
Constitutionality of the Canine Sniff Search: From
Katz to Dogs.
68 Marq. L. Rev. 57 (1984)

Comment,
Inverse Liability of State of Wisconsin for De Facto
Temporary Taking as Result of Erroneous
Administrative Decision: Zinn v. State.
1984 Wis. L. Rev. 1431 (1984)

Comment,
Scope of First Amendment Protection for Political
Boycotts: Means and Ends in First Amendment
Analysis: NAACP v. Claiborne Hardware Co.
1984 Wis. L. Rev. 1273 (1984)

Comment,
Widmar v. Vincent and the Public Forum Doctrine:
Time to Reconsider Public School Prayer.
1984 Wis. L. Rev. 147 (1984)

Comment,
Fourth Amendment Searches and Seizures, Plain
View Doctrine: Texas v. Brown.
67 Marq. L. Rev. 366 (1984)

Comment,
State v. Dean: A Compulsory Process Analysis of
the Inadmissibility of Polygraph Evidence.
1984 Wis. L. Rev. 237 (1984)

Harrington,
Right to a Decent Burial: Hazardous Waste and Its
Regulation in Wisconsin.
66 Marq. L. Rev. 223 (1983)

Jansen,
Media Access to Evidentiary Materials: United
States v. Edwards.
1983 Wis. L. Rev. 1455 (1983)

Rooney,
Freedom of the Press: An Emerging Privilege.
67 Marq. L. Rev. 33 (1983)

Comment,
Wisconsin Recognizes the Power of the Sun: Pray
v. Maretti and the Solar Access Act.
1983 Wis. L. Rev. 1263 (1983)

Comment,
Balancing on the Brink of the Chasm. Exigent
Circumstances Exception and the Fourth
Amendment's Categorical Balancing Test in State v.
Welsh.
1983 Wis. L. Rev. 1023 (1983)

Comment,
Rediscovering the Wisconsin Constitution:
Presentation of Constitutional Questions in State
Courts.
1983 Wis. L. Rev. 483 (1983)

Comment,
Free Speech in the Military.
65 Marq. L. Rev. 660 (1982)

Comment,
What are Limits to School Board's Authority to
Remove Books from School Library Shelves?
1982 Wis. L. Rev. 417 (1982)

Patton,
Corporate "Persons" and Freedom of Speech:
Political Impact of Legal Mythology.
1981 Wis. L. Rev. 494 (1981)

Comment,
Privilege Against Self-Incrimination--Truthful
Statements May be Used in a Perjury Prosecution.
64 Marq. L. Rev. 744 (1981)

Comment,
Public and Press have First Amendment Right to
Access to Attend Criminal Trials, Which Cannot be
Closed Absent an Overriding Interest.
64 Marq. L. Rev. 717 (1981)

Daskal,
Assertion of the Constitutional Privilege Against
Self-Incrimination in Federal Civil Litigation:
Rights and Remedies.
64 Marq. L. Rev. 243 (1980)

Elliot,
Right to Keep and Bear Arms.
53 Wis. B.Bull. 34 (1980)

Wesson,
Privilege   Against   Self-Incrimination   in   Civil
Commitment Proceedings.
1980 Wis. L. Rev. 697 (1980)

Comment,
Chemical Sacraments.
1980 Wis. L. Rev. 879 (1980)

Comment,
First   Amendment-Based   Attacks   on   Wisconsin
Attendance Area Statutes.
1980 Wis. L. Rev. 409 (1980)

Article IV
Legislative Branch

Farnsley,
Gambling and the Law: Wisconsin Experience, 1848
to 1980.
1980 Wis. L. Rev. 811 (1980)

Article VII
Judiciary

Heffernan,
State of the Judiciary: Court System Strives to
Maintain Effectiveness in Changing Environment.
59 Wis. B.Bull. 10 (1986)

White,
Law Clerks Would Improve Case Flow.
59 Wis. B.Bull. 36 (1986)

Brown,
Allocation of Cases in a Two-Tiered Appellate
Structure: The Wisconsin Experience and Beyond.
68 Marq. L. Rev. 189 (1985)

Ahlgrimm,
Supreme Court Rule 35:   Judicial Rotation.
57 Wis. B.Bull. 23 (1984)

Deehr,
Court Administration.
57 Wis. B.Bull. 49 (1984)

Wollenzien,
Chief Judges - Their Power and Authority Created
by Court Reorganization in 1978.
57 Wis. B.Bull. 35 (1984)

Scott,
Lawyers Respond Favorably to Expedited Appeals
Program.
59 Wis. L. Rev. 463 (1983)

Wilson,
Discretionary Review by the Wisconsin Supreme
Court.
56 Wis. B.Bull. 16 (1983)

Comment,
Statute Allowing Substitution of Judge Upon
Peremptory Challenge Does Not Violate Separation
of Powers Doctrine.
66 Marq. L. Rev. 414 (1983)

Moser,
Populism, a Wisconsin Heritage: Its Effect on
Judicial Accountability in the State.
66 Marq. L. Rev. 1 (1982)

Bukowski,
"Inherent Power" of the Court--New Direction?
54 Wis. B.Bull 22 (1981)

Article X
Education

Comment,
Rediscovering the Wisconsin Constitution:
Presentation of Constitutional Questions in State
Courts.
1983 Wis. L. Rev. 483 (1983)

LeRoy,
Egalitarian Roots of Education Article of Wisconsin
Constitution: Buse v. Smith Criticized.
1981 Wis. L. Rev. 1325 (1981)

Article XI
Corporations

Schilling,
Municipal   Debt   Finance: An   Outlook   for   the
Eighties.
63 Marq. L. Rev. 539 (1980)

Article XIII
Miscellaneous Provisions

Moser,
Populism, a Wisconsin Heritage: Its   Effect   on
Judicial Accountability in the State.
66 Marq. L. Rev. 1 (1982)

WYOMING

Chapter Fifty
WYOMING CONSTITUTION - 1890

Article I
Declaration of Rights

Keiterz,
An Essay on Wyoming Constitutional Interpretation.
21 Land & Water L. Rev. 527 (1986)

Comment,
Constitutional   Law--Does   the   New   Death
Qualification Standard Ensure a Biased Jury?
21 Land & Water L. Rev. 579 (1986)

Brinkerhoff,
Prosecution   as   a   Juvenile   or   an   Adult?   Is   the
Discretion   Vested   in   the   District   Attorney   by
Section   14-6-203(c)   of   the   Wyoming   Statutes
Unconstitutional and Violative of the Proper Role of
a Prosecutor?
19 Land & Water L. Rev. 187 (1984)

Comment,
Constitutional   Law   -   A   Constitutional   Right   of
Access to State-held Information.
19 Land & Water L. Rev. 719 (1984)

Randolph,
Characteristics, Dispositions, and Subsequent Arrests
of Defendants Pleading Insanity in a Rural State.
11 J. Psychiatry & L. 345 (1983)

Article II
Distribution of Powers

Keiterz,
An Essay on Wyoming Constitutional Interpretation.
21 Land & Water L. Rev. 527 (1986)

Comment,
Wyoming's New Instream Flow Act: An
Administrative Quagmire.
21 Land & Water L. Rev. 455 (1986)

Article V
Judicial Department

Keiter,
An Essay on Wyoming Constitutional Interpretation.
21 Land & Water L. Rev. 527 (1986)

Griffin,
Practicing Attorneys and Judicial Retention
Decisions: Judging the Judges in Wyoming.
69 Judicature 36 (1985)

Horan,
Patterns of Voting Behavior in Judicial Retention
Elections for Supreme Court Justices in Wyoming.
67 Judicature 68 (1983)

Thomson,
History of Territorial Federal Judges for the
Territory of Wyoming: 1869-1890.
17 Land & Water L. Rev. 567 (1982)

Article VIII
Irrigation and Water Rights

Mead,
Wyoming's Experience with Federal Non-Indian
Reserved Rights: The Big Horn Adjudication.
21 Land & Water L. Rev. 433 (1986)

Comment,
Wyoming's New Instream Flow Act: An
Administrative Quagmire.
21 Land & Water L. Rev. 455 (1986)

King,
Federal Non-Reserved Water Rights: Fact or
Fiction? General Adjudication of All Rights to Use
Water in the Big Horn River System and All Other
Sources.
22 Nat. Res. J. 423 (1982)

Thompson,
Statutory   Recognition   of   Instream   Flow
Preservation: A Proposed Solution for Wyoming.
17 Land & Water L. Rev. 139 (1982)

Article XVIII
Public Land and Donations

Comment,
State Participation in Federal Policy Making for the
Yellowstone Ecosystem: A Meaningful Solution or
Business as Usual?
21 Land & Water L. Rev. 397 (1986)

Lee,
An Analysis of State Energy Impact Mitigation
Programs in Colorado, Utah, Montana and Wyoming.
3 J. Energy L. & Pol'y 281 (1983)

Myler,
Mitigating   Boom   Town   Effects   of   Energy
Development: A Survey.
2 J. Energy L. & Pol'y 211 (1982)

Article XX
Amendments

Keiter,
An Essay on Wyoming Constitutional Interpretation.
21 Land & Water L. Rev. 527 (1986)

Article XXI
Schedule

Keiter,
An Essay on Wyoming Constitutional Interpretation.
21 Land & Water L. Rev. 527 (1986)

AUTHOR INDEX

AUTHOR INDEX

TITLE INDEX

TITLE INDEX

CASE NAME INDEX

CASE NAME INDEX